Around the World in 12 Years and 12 Square Meters

Memories and Insights

by Steffen P. Russak

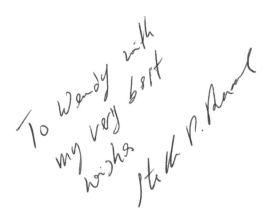

AROUND THE WORLD IN 12 YEARS AND 12 SQUARE METERS:
Memories and Insights

by Steffen P. Russak

"Suddenly, our dream of travelling the world with all comfort in a well-chosen motorhome became feasible!"

Upon retirement, Steffen and Marianne Russak set off on an epic journey around the world in a custom motorhome. This vivid travel memoir chronicles their adventure as they crisscross the globe collecting memories, living life to the fullest, and living deep in the moment every day of the journey.

Russak divides the book into two parts. The first part highlights the planning stage, shares insights into the preparations, offers advice for extended travel, and sets a mission and vision for the trip. The author is clear that they are coming from a place of gratitude and joy toward the wonders of the world and do not seek to critique countries as they pass through. The second part digs into life on the road, showcasing people, places, and specific experiences. Spanning multiple continents, this travel adventure is full of descriptive details about places and cultures but also reveals the explorers' hearts that beat strong and true in this remarkable couple.

"The story of the Russaks' adventure is a reminder that the world awaits those who still seek it out. This memoir can satisfy the longings of armchair travelers and spur others to start making their plans to get back on the world's roads."

-Michelle Jacobs
US Review of Books

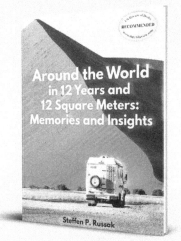

Their love for each other may only match their love for the road as the author offers this book as a tribute and moving memorial to his late wife, who passed in 2018.

Russak writes stoically about logistics and joyfully about the wonders of new places. This strong combination results in a highly readable and entertaining story that will inspire readers to hit the road in search of new adventures. He does not shy from the pitfalls, problems, and risks they encounter. From mechanical problems, accidents, and a near drowning, Russak gives an honest portrayal of the perils of driving and camping through Africa, Australia, South America, and beyond. But as natural problem solvers and seasoned explorers, they always find their way through any situation. Assuredly the joys outweigh the obstacles, and readers will feel the lure of the road and wanderlust creeping into their bones as they travel alongside the intrepid couple. As global citizens, they celebrate every corner of the world and marvel at the gifts each country offers. Russak even weaves in fables to highlight some of the worthy lessons from the world. But it's the personal stories that provide the power by showcasing the joy of discovery and the absolute commitment to living in the moment.

The travel memoir genre has a rich history as people are so often changed irrevocably by the experiences they have in new lands. Travelers are often compelled to share their stories in hopes that others will follow them across the boundaries of their cities, states, and countries out into the great unknown. These memoirs become guides that illuminate the unknown and help us see our way forward into new places. The story of the Russaks' adventure is a reminder that the world awaits those who still seek it out. This memoir can satisfy the longings of armchair travelers and spur others to start making their plans to get back on the world's roads.

Perhaps, the name the Russaks give their motorhome is the best reminder to us all of the magic of travel. Fuchur is the German name of the dragon from the film *The Neverending Story*, and it is on the back of Fuchur that the movie's young hero sees the lands of a faraway country. So, fittingly, the Russaks honor the spirit of travel by naming their motorhome after a creature known for its adventurous journeys. Thankfully, readers get to come along for the ride.

Book review by:

Michelle Jacobs
US Review of Books

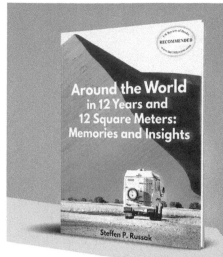

With its remarkable tales and a couple of "fables" included for pure imaginative enjoyment, Russak's large volume makes a satisfying read and a perfect "vehicle" for armchair travelers, perhaps – intentionally - inciting some to finish reading the couple's saga, get up, and go.

-Barbara Bamberger Scott
Hollywood Book Reviews

AROUND THE WORLD IN 12 YEARS AND
12 SQUARE METERS: MEMORIES AND INSIGHTS

by Steffen P. Russak

In the early 2000s, author Russak and his wife Marianne set out to fulfill a shared dream: to travel the globe in as simple, ecologically sound a manner as possible – seeking the exotic, fascinating and romantic with eyes, ears, minds and hearts open.

Russak's family are Swiss though he was raised in Brazil; Marianne hailed from northern Germany. They met at a ball in 1963 and stayed together, both nursing a lifelong yen to travel that would finally come to fruition when they were retired and ready in 2001. They initiated the process by getting the right sorts of vehicles. One was a motorbike they named Moby Dick, and the other was a custom-built motor home whimsically named Fuchur.

The specifications for Fuchur were highly complex. The rolling house was to contain a large room that could be used for relaxation and dining and quickly converted for sleeping with foldout mattresses. It would have a tiny kitchen, bathroom and closet, and a rack on the back for Moby Dick. It was many times a passenger on ships both large and small, and a dwelling in places as far apart as Australia, Brazil, Tunisia and Malawi. The pair's shared intention was to uncritically explore and enjoy.

Together they would see a million stars on a magical New Year's Eve in Chile, and the famous blooming desert of Namaqualand in Southern Africa. They would argue and cajole with bribe-seeking bureaucrats in several countries, be welcomed like family in memorable settings like the Botshabelo Mission in South Africa, and spend lazy days cruising Lake Malawi. They were once saved from death only by a small tree on the edge of a precipice when Fuchur had a mechanical failure. By an eerie chance, they met a charming guide in Tunisia who insisted on pointing out, a bit obsessively as they thought then, the way that some passages of the sacred Koran were being distorted by certain Muslims to justify dishonoring and destroying people of other faiths. Not long afterwards Steffen and Marianne saw unfolding on TV the horror of a fateful day – 9/11/2001 – and recalled the guide's weighty words.

Russak began work on this dynamic travel memoir after Marianne passed away, the book comprising his memorial to their loving, long-lasting bond. He uses some of her recollections verbatim and includes many of her brilliant and highly evocative photos. His foremost tip for like-minded rovers would probably be: Plan ahead and try to think of every possible exigency that might occur – and then, don't be surprised when something you never considered happens to thwart – or enhance – your adventures. With its remarkable tales and a couple of "fables" included for pure imaginative enjoyment, Russak's large volume makes a satisfying read and a perfect "vehicle" for armchair travelers, perhaps – intentionally - inciting some to finish reading the couple's saga, get up, and go.

Barbara Bamberger Scott
Hollywood Book Reviews

ISBN: 978-1-64314-678-2 (Hardback)
           978-1-64314-679-9 (E-book)

AuthorsPress
California, USA
www.authorspress.com

Im dedicating this book to Marianne's and my parents,
without whom nothing would have been possible,
I know that I fulfill her heart's deepest feelings
as I fulfil my own.

Around the World in 12 Years and 12 Square Meters

Memories and Insights

"Fuchur" at the Sossuvlei Dunes, in Namibia

Contents

Introduction

During twelve years my beloved wife Marianne and I travelled the world in our white motorhome "Fuchur". We enjoyed the freedom and the magnificent landscapes, marveled at Nature and its fantastic feats, at the impressive history of life on our planet and of our species in particular. But most of all we could appreciate the spontaneous kindness, friendliness and hospitality of about 90% of the people we met, regardless of origin, race, faith and station in life. Our gratitude for all good deeds bestowed on us around the globe is forever and I only regret that they were too many to be all individually mentioned in the following pages.

Marianne passed away in September 29, 2018, after a long and brave fight against cancer. Actually, we had been reluctant about writing a book concerning our years on the road, because many other globetrotters like us had already successfully published similar stories. Nevertheless, before her health got worse we had started to figure out how we could go about such a task. Now, with Marianne gone, I did start to write, concentrating on the most remarcable of those glorious days, when we were together roaming the roads of the Earth in a free, globalized world. I thus felt myself once more near that wonderful woman, my great love and faithful companion of 55 years.

Further, evening after evening I see in the news how greed, nationalism, religious intolerance, racism, antisemitism and the resulting terrorism, as well as political extremism, are conspiring to lead humanity away from a life worth living into an awful future without joy or worthy perspectives, in which globetrotters would have no place. I do hope that by telling about our experiences I am modestly helping to spread the vision of a future of freedom and happiness for our descendants.

But most of all, I do wish that you will enjoy this book and maybe someday hit the road as well… And if so, when you reach Down Under, don't miss the "Lonely Heart of Nature", visible in the turquoise waters of the Great Barrier Reef! The story of this picture I'll tell later.

PART I

The Beginnings

❖

The Origins

WHY? During the second half of the 1940s the world was starting to recover from the horrors of World War 2. In a beautiful corner of North Germany, a sweet little girl by the name of Marianne used to lie on her back, at the margins of the lovely small lake by her home and to look for the occasional airplane flying high up in the sky. She dreamed of one day sitting in such a plane to see the distant parts of the world that so aroused her curiosity.

At the same time, in the Northeast of Brazil a fanciful little boy of Swiss descent, called Steffen, sat in front of the vast Atlantic Ocean, in some tropical beach of his hometown, dreaming of hiring into one of the ships leaving the harbor, in pursuit of thousands of fascinating adventures all over the world. Later on, inspired by Jules Verne's book "Five Weeks in a Balloon" and by the Zeppelin Airships, his dream changed to one day building an airship big enough to carry a small apartment and then comfortably exploring the whole world with it.

By one of those fantastic turns of destiny, in 1963, on August 1st, the Swiss National Holyday, Marianne and Steffen met at a ball in Zurich. From that day on, the young woman from the Northern Hemisphere and the young man from the Southern Hemisphere remained together, not to part again as long as they both lived. And together they continued to dream of seeing the world, of becoming citizens of the Earth. As time went by, Steffen's dream airship landed and became a motorhome, which among others had the big advantage of allowing its passengers to keep near to landscapes, people and the rest of Creation…

WHEN? End of the 1990s it was common in the Swiss Industry for top managers to retire around the age of sixty. This practice allowed them to follow some dream while still in good health and gave ambitious younger persons the chance to climb the ladder. So in 1996 I requested and obtained permission to retire on December 31, 2000. Marianne had already stopped working as an accountant some years before, in order to cure a very seldom disorder of the immune system, which she successfully did. Now she was voluntarily driving disabled people for the Red Cross and could thus leave whenever she wanted. Suddenly, our dream of travelling the world with all comfort in a well-chosen motorhome became feasible!

HOW? As soon as I received the confirmation of my early retirement date we moved into action, in order to be ready to start our new life as globetrotters right on January 1st. 2001. There was quite a lot to be done and three years were by no means an exaggerated time frame.

Our exciting preparations took place along several stages and the final outcome was very surprising, as a result of some radical changes and improvements to our original ideas. During these three busy years we naturally lived with great expectations but, I must confess, also with a pint of regret for the distance that we would be putting from family, friends and dear little Switzerland, so richly blessed. Later, however, this distance was substantially reduced by the fact that every year we actually spent a couple of months in Switzerland, leaving Fuchur for a while under the care of trustworthy people, wherever we happened to be staying then.

A Dream Comes True

When we started our preparations for a life in a motorhome, we were experienced travelers in the usual way: by car, bus, train, airplane and ship. We were also experienced campers, having camped since our youth in all types of tents throughout Western and Eastern Europe, as well as in Brazil. Our experience with motorhomes however, was limited to a ten days tour of Florida in a rented RV. Thus, our first move was very clear:

Stage 1: the search for information

With my early retirement day fixed three years in advance, we immediately started to look out for books from people who had already done what we were about to do, which we read and discussed with utmost care. The same we did with all sorts of specialized magazines. Further, we went to all exhibitions and fairs taking place in Switzerland, Germany, France and Italy which had anything to do with motorhomes. We also visited many motorhome manufacturers and shops.

After a while we began a list of all features we wanted to have in our future motorhome, from which its main design characteristics slowly emerged. It would have to:

- be as compact as possible, for an easy shipment, an easy passage through narrow roads and streets, and last but not least, the possibility to use normal parking spaces.
- have good off-road capabilities.
- be comfortable enough, downright cozy, including the bed(s).
- be able to carry a lot of fuel and water.
- have a wastewater tank, so as not to wet or dirty the surroundings.

- have a chemical toilet, easy to clean.
- have all components placed inside the motorhome, protected against heat, cold, stones and vandalism.
- carry a motorcycle as a dinghy.

This last feature, we saw, could and should be dealt with early enough. Not only for us to gain some experience with it, but mainly to have it available for a proper fitting into the motorhome during its manufacturing. Therefore, I started the search for the appropriate machine already at this early stage. We soon bought a Peugeot Speedfight 100, considered at that time the best of all sport scooters, very compact but fit for two people, fast and also quite good on bad roads. We had it equipped with a windshield against insects, stones and rain, as well as with a big box, enough for two helmets. Our excellent mechanic installed it all and also modified the mirrors, which had to be easily removable for a better fit inside the motorhome. Marianne named this scooter "Moby Dick" (don't ask why…). With it we had great fun from the beginning, including some wonderful tours around Switzerland and Germany.

Finally the day came when we considered our basic design and the additional list of desired features complete enough for us to start looking for THE motorhome.

Stage 2: The Munga

A long search for an adequate motorhome followed. Unfortunately, we could not find any readymade or easily adaptable product that would meet our basic design as well as all our listed features. It became evident that we would have to have our dream motorhome custom made.

The next step was to find an appropriate vehicle on which to build our mobile home and one came immediately to our both minds: the DKW Munga jeep, developed after the Second World War for the new army of the new West Germany. In 1997 it was still available, but only as second–hand. It had a permanent 4WD, a reduction for  extra power, a 2-stroke engine that could burn all kinds of combustible and a special very robust suspension that was also quite comfortable. As an extra bonus, if necessary it could run on 3 wheels! We had owned one for ten years in Brazil (see picture), which we sold to a collector when moving back to Switzerland, and so knew how remarkably reliable it was. We immediately went to Germany and managed to buy one in very good shape, the biggest Munga version.

But even the largest Munga was still just a jeep and it wasn't really easy to place all our desired features on it! After some hard brain work we finally managed to find an acceptable cabin layout. Very proud of our solution we once again contacted a whole lot of motorhome manufacturers, looking for one adequate to carry out our design, but initially without success. The big ones would stick to their standard products, agreeing only to small modifications on them. The smaller ones, who would be willing to follow our design, did not seem very competent. Finally, near Stuttgart, Germany, we came to a specialized company, which was ready to build according to our plans and also made a serious, very able impression on us. We then deposited Munga and "Moby Dick" with them and hoped for the best.

They soon went to work and called a few days later, asking for us to come by. We went, feelings a bit worried and indeed were met with rather bad news, we had found a place for every feature we wanted, but the total weight exceeded by far the capacity of the Munga. We then had to decide, whether to cancel a part of our features list (including the scooter) or to replace the Munga by another, bigger vehicle.

The specialists had a suggestion. They took us to the workshop, and showed a job they were doing for another customer, converting a Mercedes "Vario" 512 D KA, actually a big delivery van, into a motorhome. This vehicle was very compact but also very spacious inside, especially due to the fact that the walls went up absolutely vertical, making it possible to have big cabinets under the roof, all around it. The specialists also pointed out that living together in a motorhome for a very long time could be stressful and that some space to move around made life easier. Further, they told us that their company had a very big discount with Mercedes-Benz, which they would transfer fully to us. Another interesting aspect was the many different Vario versions, from which to choose.

In a nutshell, the Vario would allow for all our desired features and give us more comfort than the Munga, but less off-road capability. Fortunately we could cope with the price increase. All in all, our basic design and the features we had worked out were our primary goal and the Vario was the best compromise. So we decided then and there to sell the Munga again and to go for the Vario. The Munga we sold without losses.

Stage 3: the making of "Fuchur"

Marianne, with her flair for interior architecture, became the coordinator for the living quarters, while I, the mechanical engineer, coordinated vehicle and technique.

Mercedes-Benz supplied an extensive written form with which I could choose in detail the Vario version most adequate for our motorhome. The AWD (All Wheel Drive) version proved to be not only very expensive, but also very uncomfortable (hard suspension) and maintenance intensive. I therefore settled on a compromise: a Vario with a bloc-differential that in difficult terrain can be engaged to lock the two rear wheels together. A 2WD instead of a 4WD, that later proved to be quite effective, giving the Vario pretty good off-road capabilities. An electrical winch, that we had already foreseen, gave us additional off-road resources. For occasional real tough terrain we could, if indeed necessary, try to rent an AWD and so also spare the Vario some

damages. As a matter of fact, although very robust, our motorhome wasn't built as an authentic off-roader anyway.

We had to wait a few weeks for the Vario to be delivered, but then the work proceeded quite efficiently. As it progressed, several new ideas popped up and were implemented, resulting on some very welcomed improvements. We also used this time to obtain truck driver licenses, necessary because the Vario weighed more than 3.5 tons, the European limit for the normal driving license.

A remarkable design by the manufacturer was the system to move the scooter into the garage and out of it, with the help of a small hand operated crane. The scooter could thus be easily fitted inside the garage. There was still enough space between the scooter and the door of the

garage for a plastic bag (blue in the picture) containing the windshield and the one mirror that had to be removed in the process.

Another unusual problem had also to be solved in an unconventional way. All the household technique was placed under the bed and we needed an easy and fast access to it. Several complicated solutions were under discussion when Marianne came up with the right one. She had discovered a Swiss company that produced slatted bed frames and india rubber mattresses, all of which could be easily rolled up. Whenever access to the "house" technique was needed, the thin mattress and the two frames could be rolled up and deposited on the driver and co-driver seats, as shown in the picture, or the mattress could be folded over one of the frames and the other frame removed. It is remarkable that the bed, in spite of its simplicity, was still extremely comfortable!

The next two pages show a plan of the living quarters and a detailed overview of our motorhome's features

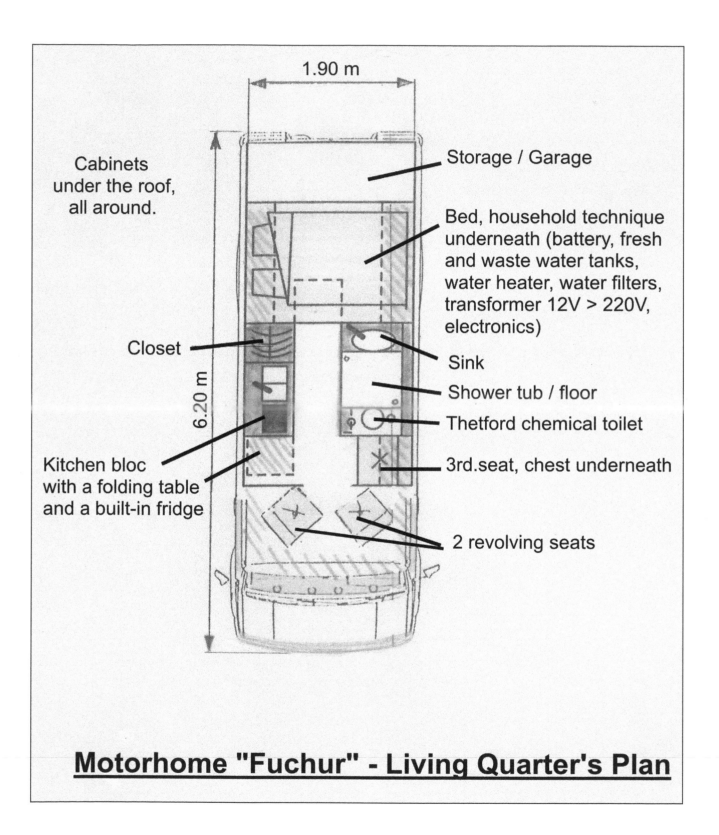

1.90 m

Cabinets under the roof, all around.

Storage / Garage

Bed, household technique underneath (battery, fresh and waste water tanks, water heater, water filters, transformer 12V > 220V, electronics)

Closet

6.20 m

Sink

Shower tub / floor

Thetford chemical toilet

Kitchen bloc with a folding table and a built-in fridge

3rd.seat, chest underneath

2 revolving seats

Motorhome "Fuchur" - Living Quarter's Plan

Motorhome „Fuchur" - Features

Size: External: 7m (23') long, 2,2m (7') wide, 3m (10') high.
Living quarter's area: 12 m² (130 ft²)

Weight: 4,8 Tons.

Vehicle : Mercedes-Benz 512D KA „Vario"; built in 2000; total distance travelled 220'000 km (137'000 miles); rear wheel drive; bloc-differential for difficult terrain; special big wheels (16"); 3 spare wheels; 1 electrical winch; chains and aluminum plates for sand, mud, ice and snow; 2 interconnected 60L (16 gallons) diesel tanks (approx. a 1'000 km/620 miles range). Driver and co-driver revolving seats, a fixed seat with a chest underneath on the driver's side, all with safety belts. Tow bar. Rear view camera." Bullgrid" in front..

Finish: All in wood, dividing walls screwed, not glued, thus easy to change. Excellent temperature and sound insulation. All doors and windows equipped with alarms and inside latches, the windows also with blinds and insect screens.

Kitchen: One 12V compressor fridge, one 2-flame stove running alternately on methylated spirits or external power, one stainless steel sink with a mixer tap for hot and cold water.

Bath/WC: A Thetford chemical toilet, a plastic sink with a mixer tap comprising an extendable shower head, a fiberglass shower tub as floor. A beach shower is located at the rear.

Bedroom: One fixed double bed with a rollable slatted frame and an india rubber mattress 1,90m (75") X 1,50m (59").

Radio/TV: Radio, DVD, TV and video recorder, all for 12V.

Heating: Two WEBASTO diesel heaters, one for water and one for air. The water heater can also alternatively run on external power instead of diesel.

Cooling: Besides the vehicle own air conditioner, a big, reversible roof fan in the bathroom and several internal fans.

Water system: One 250L (66 gallons) fresh water tank, one carbon and one biological filter, one 100L (27 gallons) waste water tank.

Power supply: One 12V Battery, charged either by 4 solar panels, the vehicle engine or external power; an electronic device automatically manages the priority. The motorhome is totally gas-free and thus independent of the entirely different local connections and standards.

Accessories: Except for an awning and some floodlights, all inside the vehicle (household technique under the bed), thus protected against heat, cold, stones and vandalism.

Storage space: In the back a 75 cm (30") deep storage compartment, initially also used as a garage for a motorbike.

Roof access: Only internally, by means of a telescopic ladder from the bed top through the open roof window. When not in use, the ladder is folded through the roof window and fixed to the roof, then packed inside a plastic cover.

The Vario needed a name and again Marianne came up with something good. She noticed that its front looked a bit like the face of the good white dragon in the film "The Never Ending Story", who carried the boy Bastian, the hero of the film, all over the country of

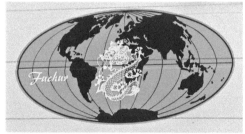

Fantasia. The name of this dragon was "Fuchur", which we adopted. Later, during a business trip in China, I bought a beautiful scissor-cut paper dragon, which served as a model for part of our Fuchur's "logo". One of our objectives was for Fuchur to look as inconspicuous as possible, like a delivery van.

Another feature worth commenting was the energy supply. Standard wise, motorhome living quarters receive power from a 12V battery that is charged either by the vehicle alternator, from the net when possible (in a camping for instance), from a small gas or diesel generator or from solar panels. An electronic manager determines which source is used, based on given

priorities: the alternator when the motorhome motor is running, the net when available and the motor is shut off, one of the other external sources mentioned in all other cases. We renounced a generator in favor of solar panels. The specialists calculated that we would need two panels, but I decided to use the whole space available so that finally we had four panels installed. It was a good decision that made us electrically self-sufficient in a 100% ecological way. Our battery kept the charge at a

useable level for at least 24 hours, even after a cloudy day (today's panels are already much more efficient than ours were!). Our battery had to feed all lamps, fans, laptops and so on, including the big compressor fridge, but not the stove (see "kitchen" at page 11).

By the way, in practice it would not be always possible to keep Fuchur in a perfect horizontal position, neither along bad roads nor in every parking space. For this reason we had to choose a compressor fridge, which works independently of the vehicle's inclination. Car inclination had to be taken into consideration also in the bath/WC (see picture), by placing two drain holes on opposite corners of the shower tub (not shown in the picture). Used water was pumped from the drain holes to the waste water tank. The picture also shows the open (mirror) cabinet door, the neon lamp on top of it and the circular porthole for the roof fan.

After the conclusion of the conversion work, we drove to a Mercedes-Benz workshop and replaced all the original wheels with 16" ones, the biggest possible according to Mercedes. They also gave us lists of the spare parts and of the tools they recommended for a trip as we had in mind, which we bought.

Upon leaving the Mercedes workshop, we happened to pass by a neighboring TÜV (the German traffic department's technical division) weighing station and decided to check our weight. Even without our personal belongings and food supplies, we were already 0.3 tons above our maximum allowed total weight of 4.8 tons! The TÜV people were very considerate and just recommended that we see how best we could reduce our weight. We however were really, really mad. It must be known that I had specified the 6 ton Vario version, but the specialists had then called and insisted on the 4,8 ton one. They said that they had calculated the total final weight very thoroughly and that with a 6 ton Vario we would be "swimming" on the road. Well, now we were "drowning" into a mess. I drove off the TÜV weighing station while Marianne immediately called the manufacturer, explained in a not exactly friendly tone the situation and got the incredible, obviously seriously meant answer: "we never expected you to take along such heavy pressure pans as you did"… At that Marianne was naturally so shocked that, at a loss for air and for an adequate answer, so she just said: "that's totally absurd, we will discuss it later!" and hung up.

The next action was Fuchur's import into Switzerland and its registration at the Swiss road traffic licensing department. All went well and now we had all number plates we needed: two for "Fuchur", one for "Moby Dick". During the technical check-up Fuchur was fortunately not weighed. Only the very high import taxes disappointed us. Later we bought two sets of copies of our new Swiss

number plates. Outside Switzerland we then replaced the originals with copies, because we had been warned against people who stole plates of different countries for their collections! The original number plates and the set of copies not in use we hid inside Fuchur. One of the copies of the rear number plate (the colorful one) later remained in the famous "Sign Post Forest" in Watson Lake, Canada, on the Alaska Highway.

Now, we drove back to the manufacturer to discuss the weight problem and for a couple of last adjustments before a longer test drive to Tunisia. It was not surprising that our discussions on the overweight issue were very difficult. The specialists reasoned that during manufacturing we had constantly added stuff to the motorhome. We argued that when I insisted on the 6 Ton Vario they assured us that the 4.8 Ton version had enough reserve for additions and never warned us when we added stuff. They assured us that ALL motorhomes run with overweight, that this was well known and no authorities would bother us because of it. At the end we had only two alternatives: accept the overweight or take legal action against the company. We did not wish to spend time and money during our retirement on a maybe long process with an unknown outcome and so opted, with great regrets, for the first alternative.

However, before accepting the overweight for good, we went to Mercedes to discuss the matter with them and managed to talk to the designer of the Vario himself. He explained to us that, due to the several reinforcements I had ordered with the vehicle, Mercedes could increase the nominal maximal weight to 5 Tons, but for legal reasons not more. However, he said, the Vario was able to take an overweight of up to 2 Tons without us even noticing it, so we shouldn't worry. We then decided to leave it at that. Indeed, Fuchur was never weighed by any authority at all, but during our trips we were always a bit worried whenever passing an official weighing station…

In January 2001 I slipped on ice in a very steep street and snapped a muscle above the right knee. So, only in the summer 2001 could we finally make our test drive: first on the direct road along the whole of the Italian boot, from the Alps to Sicily, then on a ship to Tunisia, followed by the exploration of that country.

After shipping back to Sicily, we drove north, this time along the beautiful West Coast of Italy and spent a week with our children and grandchildren in a beach camping by the Ligurian Sea. During this whole trip we could thoroughly test our Fuchur, in the mountains and in the desert, which lead to USD 5,000.00 of additional improvements and a huge amount of warranty repairs.

After seeing all our efforts to acquire a motorhome in which we could effectively live, you may be asking yourselves what the hell we wanted with "headquarters". As a matter of fact, in Switzerland we could have obtained a "globetrotter" status that would free us from paying taxes. However, this would also prevent us from

- keeping our Swiss health insurance and
- registering our vehicle in Switzerland.

We could try an international health insurance, but these are not only very expensive, they would certainly refuse to cover our existing ailments. As for the vehicle registration, we would have to drive with a false number plate, a very, very big problem in case of an accident.

Further, considering our age and the possibility of a big car accident, we wanted to be able to fly back to a home in Switzerland whenever our health may demand it. There were also administrative issues to follow up with banks, properties and so on, as well as family and friends to keep in touch with, that made it advisable for us to, once a year, park Fuchur in a safe place wherever we would then be and fly to Switzerland for a few weeks.

We were dealing with these matters in parallel with Fuchur's fabrication.

Our apartment in Winterthur, near Zurich, was too big and expensive to keep empty and we decided to choose just the furniture, pictures, etc. that we wanted to keep and to leave them in an appropriate storage. The rest we would sell or donate to a charity. A few things we planned to use in a smaller apartment that we intended to rent near the Lake of Zurich. This however proved to be impossible: the prices were extremely high and the counties demanded that we live there at least six months per year.

We had a nice holyday apartment in a beautiful ski area in the mountains, at Switzerland's Southeast. It was part of a big building with a great infrastructure, including a heated swimming pool and a roof terrace with a fantastic panoramic view. But when not being used by us during the holyday seasons, it was very profitably rented through the building's administration, with no work for us, and we didn't want to change this scheme. Besides, we wanted something really private and always available to us, which we could occupy any time we needed, independently of eventual tenants.

Sometimes, when you don't have a solution to a problem, you better just wait and give time a chance to come up with something. And so it was then. We suddenly heard that a very small apartment was for sale for an extremely low price in the same building where we had our holiday apartment. I was not interested but Marianne argued that we should have a look anyway, "It costs as much as a garage!" she said. We went and were astonished. It was very cozy, had a perfect little bathroom and one whole wall was practically a window with a great view through a forest to a small lake, the same view we loved in our big apartment. Singing birds, squirrels, rabbits and deer could be heard or seen throughout the day. And it had a cellar almost as big as our other apartment's one. Marianne immediately started to explore the full possibilities it offered, using all the experience we had been gathering in motorhome design. By coincidence this apartment had the same surface as Fuchur's living area: 12 m² (130 ft²). We bought it.

Marianne, together with a very good carpenter, set to work and in a short time had that tiny place transformed into a very cozy nest containing all we needed and wanted, without being cluttered. Our original idea of using the small apartment only if the big one was occupied soon died out and later, when in Switzerland, we only used the 12 square meters. The big apartment became a sort of hotel for our visitors, otherwise for paying guests.

During our travels in the following years we settled in a routine of visiting Switzerland only in summer, because then it was winter in the South Hemisphere, where we travelled with Fuchur most of the time. So, in fact, during 12 years we lived practically always in summer and in 12 square meter homes!

Another advantage of this small apartment was that we could concentrate all our affairs–like banks, tax matters, a trustee office and health care—in a small ski resort where everybody knew everybody else and things were kept simple, easy to handle even from afar.

A critical look backwards

Before I go on with my story, I would like to answer a question we often hear: if we were to start once more with our life as what the Australians call "Gray Nomads", would we again proceed exactly as we did the first time?

Yes, we would, except for the following modifications to Fuchr:

- *Weight* had been a painful issue for us: first I blundered with the weight on the Munga and then the manufacturer blundered on Fuchur's total weight. For a "Fuchur 2" we would stick to the Vario, but this time surely to the 6 Ton version.

- *Engine-brake*. I had underestimated the amount of downhill driving ahead of us and relinquished an engine-brake system. Although Fuchur managed even the Andes quite well, on many occasions it took some care and concentration to prevent overheating the brakes. In a new Fuchur an engine-brake system would be certainly included.

- *Household Battery*. Fuchur left the workshop equipped with two very heavy batteries for the household energy supply. In Australia we had problems with that. An expert explained that one battery was totally exhausted while the other one was still completely charged, as new, because a relatively expensive electronic manager was missing. This manager would have been needed to adequately balance the charging of the two batteries and their output. But since batteries don't fail suddenly and we had the necessary gauges to follow up its state, one battery was enough for us. We then got rid of the damaged one, a considerable weight reduction. "Fuchur 2" would therefore have only one single household battery from the start.

- *Fridge size*. We had chosen the biggest fridge we could get, thinking that we would for sure need it. Practice however, showed that we seldom used even half of its capacity. A much smaller fridge would have been enough. Then the kitchen block could have been made narrower and the space between it and the bath/WC wider, an improvement in comfort.

- *Fridge cooling*. In Australia we ran into real heat for the first time and soon the fridge went on strike. A technician found out that it was getting too hot. We then replaced the solid wood cover on its back by a wooden grid and with the resulting good ventilation the problem was solved. In a new motorhome this would be done at fabrication.

- *Roof access*. The roof platform, our "2nd floor terrace", was a feature that proved to be rather superfluous. In the African National Parks, where we had anxiously expected to make great use of it, the rangers soon informed us that it was forbidden to sit there: too dangerous! Therefore, the roof access through the roof window was actually unnecessary.

Besides, this window's rubber seal demanded constant attention and frequent vaseline applications in order not to dry out and become leaky. So, in a new Fuchur we would relinquish a roof platform and use a permanently closed roof window over the bed (but still no windows in the walls, for privacy, as well as for good temperature and sound isolation!). For ventilation, the roof fan opening over the bath/WC proved to be absolutely sufficient.

- *TV-antenna*. Fuchur was delivered with a very sophisticated TV-antenna, running through the roof. We soon found out that this antenna only worked in Europe. Already in Greece we only received Italian programs and in Turkey the reception was nil. In Australia we threw away this expensive piece of equipment and bought a simple, cheap internal antenna that served us very well for the rest of our travels. With it we could even follow all the soccer games of the 2006 World Championship out of Mozambique and Malawi.

- *Heating*. In real cold nights the Webasto diesel heater with hot water circulation was not sufficient for the whole interior. In New Zealand we added a Webasto diesel air heater, placed under the co-driver seat. This system was totally satisfactory and would be enough even alone. So, "Fuchur 2" interior should be heated just with a diesel air heater.

- *Shower tub*. The original plastic one, which was also the bath/WC's floor, started to crack after only six months of use. In Australia we replaced it, only to have the same problem six months later. As a consequence, before leaving for our next visit to Switzerland, we had the damaged tub removed by a specialist who, during our absence, used it as a model for a copy in fiber glass. Upon our return to Down Under the new tub was installed and we never had that problem again. Another thing to be considered in a new Fuchur.

- *Hanger closet*. After nine years on the road, we needed for the first time our real elegant clothing, which had been hanging in our hanger closet. It was quite a shock to see that it had been seriously damaged by rubbing against each other and against the walls of the closet. We later transformed our hanger closet into one with boards, in which we stored our "good" stuff folded and protected inside plastic bags. Naturally this experience would flow into a new motorhome.

- **Fuse box**. The original fuse box proved not to be safe enough, especially against the vibrations on bad roads. In New Zealand we had it replaced by an adequate one and in a new Fuchur we would make sure to have the right fuse box installed from the start.

- **Garage/Storage**. In Africa we very seldom used our scooter "Moby Dick", because we were afraid of leaving Fuchur alone, even in an occasional camping. This resulted in us having some trouble to start the scooter after long idle periods. We expected this problem to be even bigger in Latin America, with the huge wave of criminality in most of its countries. So, when in its way from Cape town to Buenos Aires Fuchur changed ships in Antwerp, we removed Moby Dick, took it back to Switzerland and had boards installed in the former garage that then became a very convenient storage room. However, we did miss that scooter very much, mainly when we reached USA and Canada. So that, in spite of the problems we experienced in Africa, a "Fuchur 2" would surely have a garage with a scooter in it and not a storage room.

Two other later, technically interesting, improvements I shall explain in the next chapter, when dealing with the workshops we used under way.

On October 8, 2001, we said good bye to my mother and while we were still drying our tears, Fuchur finally crossed the Swiss-German border near Basle, heading then to the manufacturer's workshop for some final touches, before on October 10, 2001 we finally drove east, towards the realization of our half-a-century old dream.

Aluminum plates for sand/mud
fixed to the right rear door

Four solar panels, roof fan opening, roof
window, packed telescopic ladder, roof platform

Storage Space, former garage

Kitchen right, Bath/WTC Left

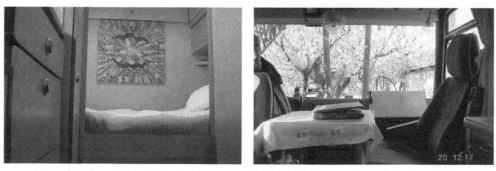

Internal backward view to the bed   Folding table between the revolving driver/codriver seats

Life in Fuchur

The occurrences I am going to present later can be much better understood if the reader is familiar with our lifestyle and with the conditions in our mobile home. By describing these now, it won't be necessary to explain them again and again, each time that they become important to the narrative.

To start with, I must make very clear that we were not on a mission of any sort! We were not trying to represent any country or organization, nor were we missioning for any faith. Neither were we trying to improve the world, to fight misery or injustice. We did and I still do think that there are enough "good people" messing around and creating more problems than the ones that already exist. The important, crucial, complex support and help activities should be left for the professionals trained to handle them. Marianne and I had both worked very hard in our lives to achieve what we had and just wanted to enjoy some of our remaining lifetime. By admiring and loving the wonders of this world we felt a little like praying and thanking the Creator for it all. So, from the beginning we also agreed NOT to engage in the frequent tourist "sport" of criticizing and reviling the countries and cultures we met. Not even were we to compare them with each other, but—out of curiosity—we just researched their history, looking for explanations to their present. Dear reader, it is your good right to consider this attitude naïve or egoist, but it is our good right as well to be happy with it. I can assure you, that it brought us some wisdom and lots of friendship. And, I am naïve enough to believe that we made a tiny, tiny contribution for a better understanding among some nations.

Dangers and disagreeable situations are an integral part of the adventure that a world motorhome travel really is. However, truthful to our purpose of enjoying life as much as possible, we tried to avoid unnecessary experiences of this sort. For instance, we drove around and not through Zimbabwe, especially after being warned that Fuchur looked very much like the United Nations' vans distributing food in that poor country, where food was worth more than gold, which made the vans susceptible to assaults by the desperately hungry mobs. And we only drove through Colombia after obtaining trustworthy information that momentarily it was reasonably safe to do so, as long as one stuck to the Pan Americana Road. Additionally, we spent the nights near some Colombian Army garrison. We knew as well that Cartagena, the Colombian port city by the Caribbean, from where we had to ship to Panama, had always been safe.

Basically, we experienced three ways of life: moving every day from place to place, staying for a longer period of time in a nice spot of our choice, or staying in a mechanical workshop.

The pictures at the end of last chapter are meant as a helpful visualization for the following text.

Moving daily

Is what we mostly did, usually living according the routine that now follows. The simple knowledge that we could basically park our home wherever we liked and remain there as long as we wished was probably the best quality of our way of life!

Our alarm clock woke us up at 7 am, local time. After the morning toilet and a quiet breakfast, Marianne tidied and cleaned the house, while I checked the car: tires, level of the liquids in the motor compartment and in the household appliances, belts' tension, etc., occasionally fixing small items. If we had internet access and time available, sometimes we dealt with our mail and had a look at the news. Normally we left between 9 and 10 am, either just to drive on, to do some shopping or to visit some place of interest, like a special nature feature, a museum, a city or whatever.

Around noon we stopped at a convenient place, sunny if it was cold or shady, if it was hot. After a light meal we normally indulged in a short siesta. Refreshed, we then plunged into the afternoon.

At about 4 or 5 pm we started to look for a place to spend the night. The search for it was always a suspense-packed activity that could be concluded in a couple of minutes or in several hours and often hit us with surprising outcomes. There was no general valid strategy for this, the conditions varying widely for each region. Australia, for instance, was overall safe, but forbade overnight stops for motorhomes at less than "x" miles from a camping ground, "x" varying for each county. Even outside this boundary, many parking lots allowed only stops for less than a certain number of hours. So, the best was to drive into the Outback and hide from view off the road behind a boulder or in a grove of coolibah tees. New Zealand was also safe, but you had to have your motorhome certified for cleanliness towards the environment in order to be allowed to stay overnight in a parking lot. In Latin America a gasoline station and in Eastern Europe a guarded parking lot were mostly the best options. We also spent many nights in normal parking lots inside cities, "hiding" behind Fuchur's similarity to a delivery van.

Shortly after our arrival in Australia we were cheeky enough to try to spend the night in front of a camping and not inside it, trusting on our delivery van appearance… Soon a young policeman found us out. After sending us into the camping this nice and evidently highly amused young man told us that he only found us out because he had heard our TV. So, we had indeed asked a bit too much from our sound isolation. Next morning, first thing, we bought a headset with two headphones and from then on could spend the night in the middle of any city without the need to sacrifice our routine. We just had to make sure that no light shone through our windows (they all had very good shades) and that we didn't react to any knocking at the doors…

A few other overnight alternatives will be shown in the stories told later in this book.

In fact, whenever possible we spent the nights near a restaurant and/or shopping facilities. Malls and supermarkets were the ideal. This enabled us to do some shopping and to get in touch with the locals, as well as to learn to know the local cuisine. The restaurants spared us the cooking, a welcome luxury. Another luxury was, after shopping, to transfer the goods directly from the shopping carts to the fridge and cupboards!

After supper we made ourselves (extremely) comfortable. Sometimes, we first read and wrote our e-mails before accessing the internet, if an acceptable connection was available. Next, came the obligatory TV time. If there was no good TV-access or program, which was mostly the case, we saw one or two of the hundred video tapes we had bought for "a smile and a dime" when the DVD introduction pushed them off the market. Next, we got ready for bed, where we enjoyed a book or a magazine until sleep came. Bed and reading light were excellent, as were the temperature and sound isolations. Before sleep took over completely, our only window, located in the roof, provided an awesome view of any eventual moon, starry night and/or tree branches.

By the way, we had found no 12V video player in Europe, but did find one in Australia.

As for the temperature regulation, our heating and cooling systems proved to be very efficient. In hot places, while driving during the day, the car's air conditioner combined with the excellent isolation kept the interior cool. After we stopped for the night, the several fans suctioned fresh night air from the outside, while the roof fan in the Bath/WC removed the hot air. At agreeable outside temperatures, we naturally just left the windows open, as much as the local safety situation allowed. Remember, all windows were conveniently equipped with mosquito nets.

With all this comfort inside, we seldom spent the evenings outside, in spite of the very handy awning. An additional reason for this was the fact that inside we had practically nothing to arrange for the evening, except to turn around the unsurpassably comfortable Mercedes driver and co-driver seats, while outside we had to fetch the less comfortable chairs from the back storage compartment and return them later. Further, outside we had no protection against the insects. If you think this last aspect is rather "sissy", then go enjoy an outside summer evening among Scandinavian mosquitos, or even better, among Australian flies entering your nose and ears… Besides, our latched doors provided a very welcome sense of safety.

In addition to shopping, we had also to purchase diesel and to fill our water tank more or less regularly. Water we could normally tank for free from public sources, camps or gas stations, except in dry areas, like deserts and the Australian Outback. In those areas we mostly obtained water from the gas stations, sometimes even for free, by only tanking diesel if the water was included in the price. With two 60-liter (16 gallon) diesel tanks we had a good business argument… Our two built-in water filters saved us from problems with water quality. Even so, we bought drinking water whenever possible, keeping always enough of it on stock.

The chemical toilet had to be regularly emptied and refilled with water and chemicals as well. We did it in public or camping toilets when possible. In the wild we just dumped the contents in an appropriate place and used our water reserves to fill the toilet again. We were informed that just dumping the refuse is preferable to burying it, if you are using biodegradable chemicals. Before we stopped burying the refuse, we tested the dumping system and found out that the refuse completely decayed to ashes in just a few hours after being dumped!

Internet access could be a problem. When we started traveling there was no Wi-Fi. Later it was introduced, but its availability spread out only very slowly. An internet cafe was mostly the best alternative. In desperate cases, access through a cellular phone was a viable option, although extremely expensive. Once we were charged over USD 2,000.00 for cellular internet connections from Greece! With the introduction of SKYPE the situation improved considerably: at one time we accessed the internet out of remote Argentinian Patagonia with skype, over the Wi-Fi of a communications center run by the Argentinian Navy, for a very reasonable price. Towards the end of our travels we started to look for restaurants or hotel parking lots with Wi-Fi access and were often successful.

Particular aspects of our travels were the shipments. Not only the intercontinental ones, in which

Fuchur was parked on and strapped to an open flat-rack container (standard, closed containers were too narrow). Short shipments over rivers, lakes or ocean stretches, using ferry boats, barges or rafts, were

also often quite special. See also the pictures at pages 14 and 20. Each one of these shipment varieties was an adventure, the risks naturally increasing the smaller the boat and the rougher the waters were…

Last but not least, I must point out that Marianne was not only a good truck driver, very careful and thinking ahead. She was also a great navigator that, with a compass and a map or street plan, could take us any place. GPS was of no use in most countries we drove through, because in them the data fed into the GPS was totally unreliable. So, whenever orientation was difficult, like in cities, I always drove and Marianne navigated! Further, she was our perfect travel guide, finding out in advance all about the places of interest ahead of us. For this purpose she mostly used the "Lonely Planet" guidebooks.

Enjoying a great place

Moving daily is fascinating; it is the very expression of the explorer's soul. As rightly said in a famous Australian country song, you always want to know what the next road curve will bring. But the human brain can only handle so much new impressions in a certain period of time and once in a while the traveler has to stop in order to assimilate all he/she has experienced along the way. Also, under some circumstances the physical exertion can be quite considerable, making a rest pause very welcome. Last but not least, sometimes a place does appeal to you so much, that you cannot resist the call to spend some time there. A few former globetrotters we met had been even bewitched into building a house and staying for life in a place like this! We did indeed always resist this temptation and at the end of our travels finally returned home for a while, before joining our children and grandchildren in the US of A.

Nonetheless, most of our longer sojourns in one place are unforgettable, either because of the beautiful surroundings, the friendly, interesting people or both. When such a place happened to be a camping or other location with a similar infrastructure, we had power, water and a permanent connection from the wastewater tank to a sewer, as well as adequate facilities for dealing with the chemical toilet. We then opened the awning and parked the bike Moby Dick nearby, ready to start any time we needed it. Because Fuchur was immobilized, Moby Dick became our normal means of transportation. See picture at page 20. In such a case I used to start Fuchur's engine once a week and let it run for about half an hour, to keep it in good shape.

If the place we chose to stay did not have the infrastructure of a camping, we obviously adapted to the resources available. Please remember that due to solar power Fuchur was energetically independent and all its tanks were over dimensioned, sufficient for longer periods of time.

In all cases above, our morning and evening routines remained similar to the ones described in "Moving daily", but during the day we engaged in many different activities, according to our moods and disposition: swimming, walking, making excursions with Moby Dick, sleeping, reading, shopping, cutting films or working with our pictures, visiting museums and so on. Sometimes friends visited or the other way around.

When staying at a beach, the shower we had at the back, inside the garage/storage, proved to be a great idea!

A situation that became naturally more frequent as the car got older. In this connection I must point out what a very experienced TÜV (the German traffic department's technical division) expert told us. He used to travel to Chile once every year, to test the Mercedes buses running in that country for a German tourist enterprise. According to him, under the road conditions in Latin America, Africa and so on, the actual age of a vehicle had to be tripled, meaning that 100,000 miles in the mentioned regions aged a vehicle like one running 300,000 miles in Europe! By this count, our Fuchu's odometer showed about 140,000 miles at the end if our travels, but its wear and tear should correspond to about 420,000 miles in Europe. However, I am very proud to stress that after our return to Switzerland and a complete service by European mechanics the car passed all official controls as new, thanks to the care and frequent services in Mercedes workshops we always gave it around the world. (Please excuse my bragging: I am just a proud parent…). We then sold Fuchur for a reasonable price to a young couple planning themselves to start a trip of their own around the world.

Anyway, we had to live very often in workshops, not only because hotels would be quite expensive, but also because we wanted to be able to follow up what was being done. Once again, morning and evening routines remained mostly as described above, but the day's schedule was dictated by the work to be done. Please don't think that those days in the workshops were dreary, a sacrifice. They were interesting, technically as well as humanely. We met very interesting people; some became good friends. From  them we learned a lot about their respective countries. And we did not spend the whole time in the workshop. Sometimes we had to wait for spare parts, for instance, and used the time to explore the area, often with a car supplied by the workshop management. In Chile we could even participate in folklore dances the employees and their families organized in the workshop premises. In Panama we gave moral support to the workshop's soccer team and then reveled in the ensuing big party.

Last but not least, our presence in the workshops was important and prevented many mistakes, besides speeding things up. In Argentina however, our presence was forbidden for rather odd insurance reasons and there almost every service was blundered, the last one leading to costs of USD 11,000.00 in Panama: a differential gasket was mounted in reverse, leading to an extremely slow, on the dust covered parts hardly detectable leak and finally to the total differential destruction…

It is important to clarify that by workshops I mean not only the mechanical vehicle (Mercedes-Benz) workshops, but also the specialized RV facilities and others. I have already mentioned the addition of an air heater by WEBASTO, in New Zealand, the improvement of the fridge's ventilation, the replacement of the plastic shower tub with a fiberglass one and the modification of the hanger closet as examples of workshop jobs in the household area.

Further, I have mentioned two technically interesting improvements, which I would present in this chapter, and here I am. Since these jobs are purely of technical interest, readers whose passions lay somewhere else are welcome to jump over the rest of this chapter and go straight to the first story.

JOB 1: internal access ladder to the roof, running from the top of the bed and through the roof window. As already explained, we would relinquish this access in a new Fuchur. But in our Fuchur we had the roof access and originally expected to use it. We had therefore ordered an internal ladder, which our manufacturer could not supply because he didn't know how! Other workshops we kept asking along the way gave the same answer. All proposed the usual fixed external ladder which we refused: we did not want to make it easy for everybody to crawl up to our roof and peek at us in bed through our roof window…

Our manufacturer's problems had been: The ladder had to be easily removed and stored, could not damage the roof window rubber seal and could not put pressure on the rather delicate slatted bed frame. He considered the job impossible. I was sure it could be done but didn't have then the time to concentrate on an adequate design. So, we remained with the provisory solution of pulling ourselves up through the roof window by force of our arms, a stressing exercise in which we always risked damaging the rubber seal. And it was not getting easier with age.

I kept struggling without success for a solution, until we reached New Zealand. There, end of 2005, in a specialized RV-shop, I stumbled over a small metal telescopic ladder that, when

fully extended, was long enough to reach the roof without touching the bed and when totally pushed together could easily pass through the open roof window in any possible position. When I saw it "the lights went on" and I immediately bought it. I then designed a system by which that ladder could be fixed to Fuchur's roof, complying with all the demands described above. In Christchurch we found a workshop that manufactured and installed

it for about USD 7,000.00. Later in Penrose by Auckland, I had the roof reinforced (picture), because we noticed that it was flexing under our weight, especially Marianne's, bad me told her…

My design looked a bit complicated at first sight but was in reality quite simple. The ladder I had bought was attached to two square stainless-steel tubes sliding inside two other slightly wider square tubes, which were welded to the roof platform, our "terrace". The ladder attachment to the sliding square tubes was done by means of bolts, so that when not in use the pushed together ladder could be rotated through the open window, to rest outside, on top of the welded square tubes. For use, the ladder would be rotated back inside the car and then extended. In this position, supports in the sliding square tubes kept the ladder slightly inclined, so as not to touch the bed. When not in use, the sliding square tubes were slid away from the window, not to interfere with the window cover. In use, the sliding square tubes were slid back, bridging the rubber seal area that was thus kept effectively out of harm's way.

The ladder, packed in plastic, not in use

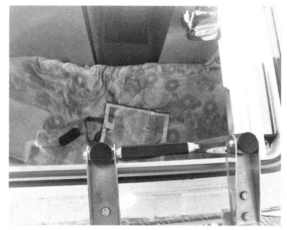

Top view, rubber seal bridged for ladder in use

Ladder in use

Enjoying the roof

Marianne and I were very happy with this system and deeply regretted that circumstances in practical life did not allow for a better use of our roof "terrace".

JOB 2: To stop the protection front grid from breaking in every bad road. This had become a real nuisance. Every time it happened, I stabilized the grid with a provisory rope arrangement and had it later welded at the next best opportunity, only to have it broken again soon after entering a bad road.

Our protection grid was an important piece of equipment, because it carried the electrical winch and one of our three reserve wheels, in addition to its protective function.

We had no problems in Europe, but as soon as we hit the Australian Outback these started and got progressively worse in Africa, culminating in Namibia with its single one asphalt road. Finally, in Windhoek I asked the Mercedes-Benz workshop to seriously take care of this issue, but they said that they didn't work with protection grids and gave us the address of THE specialist for protection grids in Namibia. This gentleman proved to be a very nice person, running together with his wife a small but very clean and well-organized company and making a very competent impression. He vehemently criticized the way our grid had been attached to Fuchur's chassis, then redesigned and rebuilt the whole thing. It really looked much better now and only broke after twelve miles of bad road, instead of the former usual ten miles…

After this disappointment I finally remembered that some people had once thought that I was a reasonably good mechanical design engineer and crawled under the car to study the situation. I found the grid firmly fixed to the chassis by four robust screws. I made neither measurements nor calculations, but my experience told me that all looked properly dimensioned. So, the problem seemed to lie somewhere else, but where? I then started to mentally review the history of the breakages and suddenly it downed on me that every time only one side of the grid had broken and afterwards nothing more happened. This could only mean that the grid gained some flexibility after my provisory repair with a rope arrangement and therefore didn't brake anymore. The reason was, that from my rope repair onwards the critical material stress which had led to the rupture had been in part absorbed by the material deformation, a well-known fact put to use mainly in airplane design.

With this insight the rest was easy. I bought four screws of the same type and diameter as the ones in use, but longer. For each screw I bought one additional nut and one additional washer. I then replaced the screws in use by the new ones and assembled these as shown in the sketch. The first nut was tightened just enough to hold the screw in place but not enough to prevent some freedom of movement perpendicular to the screw's axis. The second nut, however, was tightened as much as possible against the first nut, to surely hold it in its position. Finally, I lubricated the spaces between the washers and the grid with a teflon-based lubricant. Now the grid could move a little bit against the chassis and so allow for a small amount of deformation. Naturally the diameter (D) of the holes through the grid had to be somewhat bigger than the diameter (d) of the screws. Never again did the protection grid break. (Do I hear some applause???)

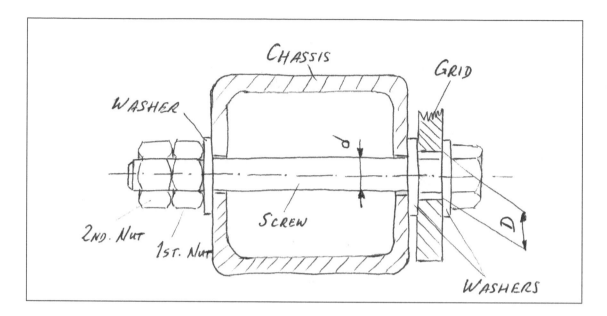

And finally, this world map roughly shows Marianne's and mine's whereabouts between 2001 and 2013

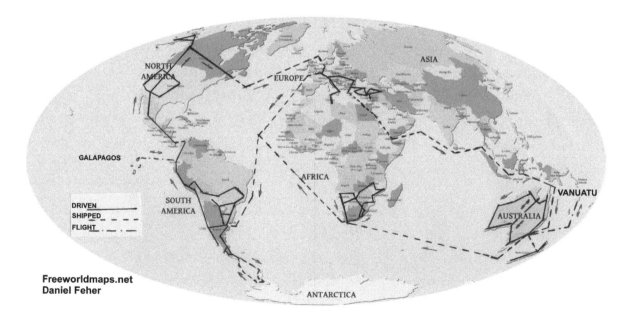

PART 2
On the Road

❖

Ushuaia

Ushuaia is the southernmost town on Earth and thus, geographically, the best harbor from which to visit the Antarctic. It is therefore no wonder that from there a huge amount of tourist ships, of all shapes and sizes, offer cruises to the impressive "Fifth Continent". Unfortunately, the quantity of tourists from all over the world, desperately willing to experience this adventure, often surpasses the capacity of even all those vessels. Quite astonishing, considering the remoteness of Ushuaia! For this reason I had not thought of buying our tickets in advance, but rather to wait for our arrival in Ushuaia and to try there to get a "last minute" cabin, maybe even for a better price. I saw in this strategy a greater chance of success.

We had shipped Fuchur from Cape Town to Buenos Aires, with a change of ships in Antwerp. This change of ships took a couple of weeks, during which we had managed to send Fuchur through some repairs and modifications. We had then flown to Buenos Aires and enjoyed that city while waiting for Fuchur's arrival. This anxiously expected event was considerably delayed, the reasons as usual unclear, and we ended up with a lot of time in our hands. This was when Marianne had one of her famous hunches, which she called her "tummy feelings". She said that our idle spell in Buenos Aires had been given us for a reason, probably for us to try to find a good Antarctic cruise. After almost fifty years of marriage I knew better than to challenge her "tummy feeling" and we immediately took action. At the seventh or eighth travel agency we finally hit the jackpot: a very congenial and also efficient lady offered us a cabin for about USD 3,500.00! The best price we had been offered until then had been something like USD 8,000.00. The reason for the low price was the cabin's location amidships, thus without windows. However, later during the cruise this cabin proved to be not only very warm and quiet, but also quite inured to the ship's movements in rough waters. Anyway, for the sights we were like everybody else, including the passengers with big windows, always on deck.

In addition to the above mentioned advantages of our cabin, in Ushuaia we found out that due to extremely bad weather two cruise ships had sunk shortly before our arrival, fortunately without deaths, and therefore the passengers booked for the future cruises of these lost vessels had been, whenever possible, distributed among the remaining ships, so that there were absolutely no "last minute" cabins to be had. The last cabins sold in Ushuaia had cost above USD 15,000.00! So, Marianne's "tummy feeling" proved once again its worth, incomparably more trustworthy than mere strategic thinking!!!

Fuchur's customs clearance in Buenos Aires was uncomplicated and speedily carried out by the friendly Argentinian officials. This was the first of many such positive personal contacts we were going to experience during our stay in that country.

Due to the approaching date scheduled for our cruise's start, we drove rather briskly down the Argentinian Atlantic Coast, along Patagonia and Tierra-del-Fuego, leaving quite a few sights to be dealt with on our drive back, after the cruise. The road to Ushuaia crosses a small stretch of Chilean territory, so that we had to pass a border control into Chile and a couple of hours later one back into Argentina. We were lucky to hit a very quiet time with few cars moving in both directions, so that reentering Argentina we were the only tourists in the border office. The friendly official in charge of the passports' control, with enough time to chat, asked us if this was our first visit to Ushuaia, which we confirmed. We then gratefully accepted his offer of some useful tips and got the most complete Ushuaia guideline possible. Among other precious information he called our attention to the "centollas", a gigantic, delicious crab that is only found around Ushuaia and in Alaska, at the same distance from the Equator. He also told us which restaurant had the best ones. Another valuable recommendation was to stay at the Camping "La Pista del Andino", which then became our next destination.

The Camping "La Pista del Andino" was run by two "muchachos porteños", meaning young men from Buenos Aires. Some years ago they had been vacationing in Ushuaia and liked the place so much, that they decided to stay for good, at least to spend most of the year there. Ushuaia is a lively, interesting place, with lots of activities going on all the time and radiating a very special atmosphere. Its charismatic "World End" location nestled between the Beagle Channel and glacial peaks reaching from sea level to almost 1500m (4,900ft) height, neighboring the fascinating "Parque Nacional Tierra del Fuego", is indeed very, very unique. So, after deciding to stay in Ushuaia the two capable young men started looking for a way to earn their living and noticed that the extensive ski area of the "Club Andino" stayed empty most of the year. A meeting with the club management ended with an agreement for them to, outside the ski season, use the club area and its infrastructure for a RV camping. Those two guys then went to work and with much engagement, as well as skilled management, created a success story. The main engine of this success was certainly their permanent presence, sympathy and creativity in solving problems, duly underlined by the typical "porteño" humor, of which I'll give an example:

Before we left for our Antarctic cruise, we moved good old Fuchur to a spot in front of the camping building containing the office, the restaurant and the young men's apartment, so that they could permanently keep an eye on it. When Fuchur was all set for our absence, Marianne and I went with our luggage to their living-room. They had kindly offered for us to stay there during the two hours before our taxi arrived. While one of them helped with the luggage and tried to make us as comfortable as possible, the other one started the TV and shoved a video into it, saying:

— *You are going to spend two weeks in a ship and so I looked for an appropriate film, to get you in the right mood.*

When the film started we couldn't believe our eyes. It was "*Titanic*"… As you will see, those two weren't the only ones thinking in this direction! There was a really weird, far reaching connection between our cruise, the Titanic and my suits, that I'll try to explain as this story unfolds. First of all I must tell about my suits.

Marianne and I had thought that for good measure we should always have with us one or two elegant garments each. For this purpose, we had squeezed in Fuchur a narrow wall cupboard between the bed and the kitchen, in which I hang two suits. Marianne had only non-ironing dresses that she folded and kept on shelves. The day before boarding the cruise ship, as we packed, heaven fell onto my head: During the nine years on the road, before Ushuaia, my never needed suits had been rubbing against each other and against the walls of the cupboard without us noticing and were now so worn out in some places as not be useable anymore! In the instructions for the cruise that we received in Buenos Aires, suits were clearly listed as a must and so we ran in desperation to our two camping managers, asking for at least one shop in Ushuaia were I could find acceptable replacements. They took this as a joke and wouldn't believe somebody really, really needed suits in our times… They said that they didn't have a clue where to find such things… Finally we could convince them to make some phone calls and so obtained two addresses downtown. To make a long story short, we found a suit and a blazer, both of very good quality but in need of some adjustments, for which a local seamstress was highly recommended to us. This good lady shoved everything else from her and plunged into the business of fitting my garments. I don't know how much sleep she had that night, but next morning she had an excellent job done, for an incredibly low price. Back to the camping with a light heart and a smile in our faces we had to satisfy the curiosity of our two friends, who inspected my new suits with a mixture of admiration and incredulity about their worthiness…

Well, after the suit's novel and the "Titanic" film we boarded the luxurious American cruise vessel "*Marco Polo*" for two excellent weeks along the Antarctic Peninsula, regardless of the cloudy, windy and rainy weather, as well as a very rough sea. There we also spent a grand New Year's Eve 2007-2008, which all by itself more than justified my new suits!

Wikimedia Commons

We visited three research stations and met with countless very tame penguins and seals. For these purposes we left the ship on rubber dinghys. Once a dinghy (fortunately not ours) had one of its air cushions damaged against some rocks and was then filled with ice cold water, an experience its passengers would have gladly missed…

A very impressive event was a tour inside the Deception Island "caldera", the crater of an extinct volcano, now filled with water, which our huge ship entered through a very narrow passage.

The "caldera"   Inside the "caldera" (entrance on top, right)

On board, besides excellent service and food, we had all sorts of social and cultural events, including lectures about every aspect of Antarctica. We also met very interesting and nice people.

Our captain, a Norwegian, was a very likeable person with a great sense of humor, who loved to tell stories that he said were true, but you were never sure if it was really so or just another sailor's yarn. The one Marianne and I liked best goes as follows: In one of his cruises there was a lovely, elderly American couple on board with whom he soon became very friendly. They used to sit or stroll together on deck and to talk about all sorts of things. One day the lady asked:

- *Captain, I note that you have a slight accent. Where do you originally come from?*
- *I am Norwegian*, says the captain
- The old lady looks at him in horror and almost screams: *But this is awful! You descent from the Vikings! They burned cities, violate all women who came their way and robbed whatever they could get their fingers on…*
- *Please don't get upset, madam*, interrupts the captain. *Things have changed a bit lately, we don't burn cities anymore!*

Aboard the ship Marianne had bought dresses and blouses that needed some fitting. Therefore, after disembarking we went straight to the seamstress we already knew. When we walked into her shop she looked at us as if she was seeing a ghost and then jumped up screaming "my tourists are back, my tourists are back!" and hugged us with tears in her eyes. We didn't know even what to think. As she slowly calmed down, we started to understand what had happened: Again a cruise ship had sunk, this time near the Malvinas Islands and apparently with deaths. She knew we were going on a cruise when we had left her, but didn't remember which and was terribly worried that we might have been in the sunken ship. I cannot begin to tell how touched we were by so much human feeling after such a short acquaintance! Somewhere deep in our DNA there is gene for love in which we must trust, in spite of all the evil around us.

By the way, we were assured that three ships sinking around Ushuaia in a short period of time were a once ever situation, due to very rough seas and much bad luck. It was said that maritime disasters are rather seldom there.

Leaving the house of our now so close seamstress, Marianne and I realized that the recent sinking of three ships really looked as if the ghost of the Titanic had cast its tragic shade upon our cruise. Fortunately without touching us, for which we thanked God. We also recognized the weird connection I mentioned before, between the Titanic, our cruise and my suits, a connection established by way of the two camping managers and the seamstress. This may seem farfetched, is certainly weird, but if you think it out you'll find it to be true.

Well, after the cruise, back to the Camping "La Pista del Andino" we were not greeted by our hosts with "welcome back, how was the cruise?" or words to the same effect, but with "did you really wear those suits?".

In spite of this, we still stayed in Ushuaia for another week, exploring its marvelous surroundings, especially the National Park. What stands out in my memories of this Park are the many beavers, my fellow engineers, and their impressive dam system that changed the whole hydrology and with it the ecology of the area.

On inspection tour

Hard work!

Top view of a beaver dam

Front view of a beaver dam

One day, while visiting that beaver neighborhood, Marianne and I were walking along a rough and winding path, talking and looking where we were stepping. I was saying something when I suddenly realized that I was speaking to the woods, Marianne was not there! Somewhat worried, I reversed direction and went in search of her. After the first curve there she was, talking to somebody. First I didn't see whom she was talking to, but then saw a big beaver sitting on the path, right in front of her, paying concentrated attention to what she was saying. In my science fiction trained imagination I could formerly see a virtual pencil tucked between his head and his also virtual ear (beavers don't have ears…) and a virtual technical drawing in his hand. In order not to disturb this remarkable "close encounter of the third kind" I remained very quiet until it finished and even forgot to at least take a picture. Now you only have my word for it, what puts me in same situation as the Norwegian captain of the "*Marco Polo*" with his stories. Damn, damn, damn!

On the way back from Ushuaia, crossing into Chile, the Argentinian border office was totally filled up with tourists, as opposed to our arrival a few weeks ago. We had to stay in a long cue and finally landed with another officer than the one who had been so kindly helpful with his Ushuaia tips. But he was still there, this time very busy with the many tourists. After getting our passports duly stamped, we somehow managed to squeeze ourselves in and to thank him once again for his kindness, which evidently made him very happy.

I hope to have been able to share with you some of that wonderful experience Marianne and I had in the southernmost continental corner of our (still) marvelous planet. In spite of the fantastic landscapes we saw and the remarkable atmosphere we felt, when in later years we remember those days, it is the people we had the pleasure to meet that first touch our hearts and thoughts. And with people I don't mean the *Homo sapiens* representatives alone.

Ksar Ouled Soltane, July 3rd, 2001

During our test drive through Tunisia, Marianne and I found out that in the past the Berbers, an old and very resourceful people, had built fortified granaries called "ksars". These consist basically of multi-level buildings, each level containing several barrel-vaulted compartments, the "ghorfas", which were rented for the storage of valuables, mainly grains and palm oil. The buildings surrounded one or more interconnected courtyards and the different levels were reached from the courtyards over external stairways. The thick walls and the total absence of openings at the external walls made the ksars practically impregnable. Defense forces could operate from the top of the buildings. Those ksars can be found all over North Africa–Morocco, Algeria, Tunisia, Libya–and were in fact the banks of the Sahara. Their customers were the locals as well as nomadic peoples like the Bedouins.

Built in the 11th century, the remarkable Ksar Ouled Soltane, with two courtyards, is located in southern Tunisia. It rises to the impressive height of four levels and had been renewed to its original condition. Further, it was still inhabited, with daily life running its normal course. We decided to pay it a visit, not even remotely suspecting that the name and date mentioned in the title above would remain forever engraved in our memories. This story will show why.

After a drive over beautiful desert landscapes we could behold, on top of a hill, the outline of Ouled Soltane, dominated by the ksar and the mosque. Once inside the village we parked alongside the mosque, near the entrance to the ksar. It was about 04:00pm. Already as we were getting out of Fuchur, a very well-mannered gentleman in the typical Berber attire came to say hallo, welcoming us in name of the village. He then offered to show us around, including the ksar. He didn't give the impression of being a tourist guide, rather that of a well-to-do citizen that had, by chance, seen us arrive and was being hospitable. We therefore accepted his offer with thanks.

A leisurely tour followed, with excellent explanations. We were very impressed with our host's profound historical knowledge and his subtle sense of humor. We finished the sightseeing in one of the ksar's courtyards and he then invited us for a tea in that courtyard itself, "to enjoy it's typical atmosphere". It was a hot day, but he showed us a very shady corner, swept by a refreshing breeze, in which the wall built

a wide seat, and asked us to wait there a moment, while he organized the tea. He returned in a couple of minutes with a chair and a cover for the seat in the wall, followed by a man bringing a round table, who a bit later also brought some delicious tea. By then we were already best friends and the open, honest conversation that ensued took an unexpected serious turn when he started to talk about his personal worries.

In the meantime, we had noticed that everybody passing by came to respectfully greet him and—because we were with him—to greet us as well. This showed us that he must have been an important person in the village, maybe the mayor or another local authority. Since he had not asked anything personal about us, we thought this may be considered rude in his environment and also didn't ask him any personal questions. We hoped he would sometime volunteer such information, but he never did. He gave us his name though, but we regrettably omitted to write it down and now, nineteen years later, I have forgotten it.

But let's get back to our new friend's personal worries. He told us that he was a very religious person, faithfully following the teachings and rules of Islam. He had been studying the Koran all his life as well as following the rule to pray kneeling towards Mecca five times a day. And now—so he said—all over the Islamic world there were false teachers, fanatics, perverting the Koran so as to justify all sorts of crimes, in fact attracting a lot of young people and actually conditioning them for a "jihad", a religious war.

At a point, he pulled a small Koran out of one of his pockets and started to translate some passages from Arabic into French and then, in an impressive demonstration, to show how by taking some phrases out of the context and combining them in a new paragraph, exactly the opposite of the Koran teachings came out. I still remember an example, in which he read the Koran saying that the Jews ("The People of the Book") and the Christians were the brothers of the Muslim and so the Muslims had the duty to explain to them the "true faith", but if the Christians and Jews didn't want to join it, they were still brothers and honored guests and should be treated as such. After some manipulations of this text, as explained above, came out that the Jews an Christians **had to** be converted by **all means**. This, our friend said, was what those fanatics taught the youngsters and even told them that they should be ready to voluntarily sacrifice their lives in this "holy" mission, which would grant them incredible delights in paradise. We got the impression that many Muslims were extremely worried and were really dreading a terrible, in their opinion possible religions' war.

In those days we had not yet heard anything about all this and were naturally very much surprised. However, while our friend was away for a moment, ordering more tea, Marianne and I agreed that he and his like-minded fellows were exaggerating, maybe making life more exciting in an otherwise somewhat boring existence. This point of view we deepened further in the days that followed and as new impressions flooded our lives, we pushed aside this part of that extraordinary visit.

Our late afternoon tea came to an end when it started to get dark and our host announced that it was time for him to go to the mosque for his last, fifth prayer of the day. However, before we said good-bye, he invited us to drive our motorhome into the courtyard and to spend the night there. He still helped us to overcome the high step at the entrance and to find the best place for the overnight. We spent a quiet evening viewing the mosque through our front window and later the

top of the buildings through the roof window over our bed. After a good night sleep, we woke up to enjoy the sunrise and, as registered by my efficient wife in her accurate notes, left at 08:15am. Our friend had asked us to leave early.

Just a little more than two months later, Marianne and I were in Schleswig-Holstein, Northern Germany, where she had been born and had grown up, to say good-bye to the family before starting our motorhome travels around the world. One morning we were enjoying a really good North German brunch at the home of one of her cousins. The whole family was sitting around a big table. One of the girls, however, had finished eating early and was now watching TV. Suddenly she stormed into the dining room, looking very pale and almost in tears, saying: "Something awful is happening in New York, you must come to the TV at once!"

It was the 09/11/2001.

I certainly don't need to stress how the indescribable scenes shown on TV and the horrible additional news filled us all with a mixture of despair, infinite sadness and—let's be frank—tremendous but impotent hate. When the shock started to ebb away, Marianne and I remembered our good friend in the Ksar Ouled Soltane and his fears that we had so arrogantly dismissed. This brought us emotionally down and back to a more reasonable state of mind. It was good to know that out there were lots of Muslims, certainly the huge majority, who were suffering like us over those incredibly barbaric acts. This insight helped us to focus our hate on the criminals who planned and executed such a thing and not to generalize against the whole Muslim population.

Since that day a lot has happened. But I still try never to think of *nineeleven* without at the same time remembering *july-three* at the Ksar Ouled Soltane.

View from the Ksar Ouled Soltane

Botshabelo

Soon after arriving in a new country where we expected to remain for a good while, we applied for membership in the national motorhome club. And so we did in South Africa, joining the MCSA (Motorhome Club of South Africa) immediately after Fuchur's arrival in Cape Town, on 04/29/2006. We were very lucky, because from 04/27 to 05/01/2006 the MCSA West Cape's

20th Rally was taking place and we were invited to join it right away! It was a huge, magnificent event and we were received with an incredible amount of sympathy and the most generous hospitality, certainly one of the great highlights of

our travels. Later on, in Johannesburg, a small MCSA delegation paid us a welcome visit and even published in their newspaper an article about our travels.

The reason I mention this, is because from those nice people, on both events, we got an awesome amount of insider information about Southern Africa, that proved of great value and made a considerable difference on our exploration of that part of the world. Among other recommendations, there was the one I wish to share with you now. It concerns the **Botshabelo Mission Station of the BMS (Berlin Missionary Society),** in which's premises also rests a **Ndebele Village & Museum**.

This Station is located near the village of Loopspruit, roughly 50 miles (80 km) East of Pretoria and is a real insiders' tip. We couldn't find it in our documents. Even in our Lonely Planet it is only inconspicuously indicated in the Map of the Mpumalanga Province but without the slightest reference to it anywhere else. No wonder that we were indeed the only visitors, fortunately I might add!

Botshabelo means "place of refuge" in the Northern Sotho language, and refers to the historical roots of the Mission, as we will see in a moment.

The Ndebele were a people of great warriors and also great artists, related to the Sothos of Lesotho and South Africa. In 1834 they occupied the South of today's Zimbabwe, where they built its most charming city, Bulawayo, as their capital. Towards the end of the 19th century, following a long war with the British colonial forces—which finally occupied the whole country, naming it Rhodesia, in honor of the famous Cecil Rhodes—the Ndebele had to accept a very disadvantageous agreement and lost their power.

In 1865 the BMS missionary Alexander Merensky founded the Botshabelo Mission, after having to abandon a former mission in the Transvaal, because of attacks from surrounding tribes. Botshabelo soon became a haven for many Ndebele people, also in need of protection from aggressive tribes. Their traditional, outstanding art works, together with their beautiful village in the typical Ndebele architecture were later combined to form the living museum we visited. The missionaries provided for a good schooling and several Ndebele became teachers, lay-preachers and artists of renown, a few artists even in Europe.

The Mission is partly surrounded by a gorgeous forested area—a national park—containing a river and small lakes, as well as housing a rich fauna: antelopes, birds, horses, monkeys and so on.

We arrived at the Mission on the beautiful afternoon of August 9, 2006 and made ourselves at home in the camping area by the river. First, we explored the area, enjoying landscape and fauna. Then we took a brief look at the beautiful village, said hello to a few people and decided to go for a long walk along the river, leaving the actual sightseeing for the next day. That walk proved marvelous and we only noticed that we had gone very far when it was already quite dark. We turned around and were suddenly surrounded by six or seven very lively, big horses! They were apparently used to humans but still pretty wild. We were a bit worried but soon noticed their friendly intentions: Each one came to us individually and wanted to be stroked. We then walked back to Fuchur together with those big guys walking right beside us. In the meantime it had become completely dark. The horses were very playful and would sometimes softly nudge our back or shoulders. After bringing us directly to Fuchur's door and "saying" good night, they spread out around the car, peacefully enjoying the soft grass they found there. In spite of all friendliness shown by those great horses, I am not ashamed to confess that we felt somewhat relieved to be inside our faithful vehicle… We could still see them when we went to bed but next morning they were gone. We always remembered that small adventure as another "close encounter of the third kind"!

After a good night's sleep we started the new day by visiting the Mission and its own museum, learning something of their history. We had to admire the buildings, all designed and constructed

by missionaries that did not have any architectural training. Afterwards we went to the Ndebele village/museum with plenty of time at our disposal. There we met with the ladies alone, because the men were out, at work. But the ladies, in their colorful attires, were the main artists and therefore the best contact for us. They willingly explained their work and didn't mind being filmed or photographed. Marianne's film camera found great interest and they did really enjoy watching her films. While the ladies were keeping themselves busy, in a very relaxed and friendly atmosphere, I went around looking at the village as a whole, with its interesting architecture and decorations.

The villagers' artwork could best be seen in their shop, were we spent quite some time and bought a few very interesting items, mostly as presents but a few for our own home as well. Then an elderly, very proud and dignified lady, certainly the wife of the local chief, wanted to see our Fuchur. We led her there, helped her to get inside and offered her a seat. She sat very upright, looked around without talking nor showing any emotion, but stayed very long, which showed us that she was in fact really interested.

She didn't accept any drink nor sweets.

After that we stayed around for a while, Marianne still chatting with the ladies. When they left for lunch we went for a short walk under the pleasant shade of the many trees. Because Fuchur was parked under the hot sun, we left the front window, at the driver's side, about 8 inches (20 cm) open, thinking that no robbery was to be expected there. A big mistake!

We always had a bunch of bananas hanging over the kitchen sink. When we returned, we couldn't believe our eyes. A relatively big monkey was sitting on the border of the sink, happily eating our bananas! He knew exactly that we were the owners of the car and was keeping his eyes on the path we had taken. As soon as he spotted us back, he grabbed one more banana, jumped to the driver's seat and slipped, we never

knew how, through that narrow window opening and sat on the ground a good distance from us. All this at an incredible speed. Then he calmly enjoyed finishing the banana he had started before we came, followed by the extra one he had taken when leaving the car. After that, with great dignity, he climbed up the next tree, sat up there and—I swear!–started laughing us out. We were at first speechless, but soon joined him in his laugh. There was nothing else we could do; we knew that the police were powerless in this case... The state in

which that monkey left our bunch of bananas you can witness by yourself in the picture at right.

With this remarkable event still bringing out a smile to our faces we said our colorful lady friends goodbye and hit the road once more.

Off the beaten track in Tunisia

(Recounted by Marianne)

We drove up a mountain road to Matmata for a visit to the underground houses typical of that region. It was in July 2001 and unbearably 42°C (108°F) hot, naturally in the shade... That scraggy landscape is inhabited by shepherds, who live there without any kind of comfort.

A friendly but somewhat uncommunicative housewife showed us her agreeably cool two rooms' cave-house. The rooms were just two holes dug into the earth, accessed from a huge round hole that was used as a courtyard and from which some other cave-houses had been dug out as well. One of the rooms was used as a bedroom, the other as a living room and kitchen. There was no running water nor electricity. In spite of these shortcomings, we immensely enjoyed the pleasantly cool cave-house kitchen. Our motorhome "Fuchur", even with the air conditioner running, was much hotter. Some dromedaries, belonging to a herd lying nearby for a nap, were also feeling the heat but still let their heads rest on the hot sand. Before we departed, I gave the husband a blouse for his wife and he gave me a bottle artistically filled with colored sand.

For the way back, our guidebook recommended an asphalt road with an impressive view over a lunar landscape, which should lead to the valley. Unfortunately, this road was interrupted due to road works. A provisory sand road without marked boundaries followed along a hillside that dropped in a steep gradient. Seldom did we meet an oncoming car. Here and there we came across a shepherd with his flock. While we vainly expected to again find the asphalt after the next curve, it slowly downed on us that we were on the wrong road. The sun was already quite low and we had no idea where we were.

Finally, at some distance from the road we saw a farm house. The driveway was too narrow for Fuchur. Because a short time ago we had been pestered by a bunch of kids who hang themselves at Fuchur screaming "stilo, stilo, stilo" (ball pen) and "chewing gum, chewing gum, chewing gum", we didn't want to leave the car alone. So, duly armed with the road map, I walked up to the farm house. The people there looked suspiciously at me, called to each other words I didn't understand and just shook their heads when I showed them the town we were looking for in the map. Well, I then went back to the car and saw how Steffen tried to turn it around, to return looking for a better road. In this process he almost got Fuchur stuck in some loose sand… And now a strong wind came up, blowing my hat away and filling my eyes with sand.

Steffen changed his mind and didn't think anymore that it was a good idea to return along the

bad road. I forgot to tell that on that bad road we had seen a car stuck deep in sand (see the picture) and Steffen had helped to push it out. So he now said that with all that loose sand we could be happy that we had gotten so far. I had an eerie feeling in that loneliness, where the few people we met did not understand us and the road was getting worse and worse. At each curve I looked down the steep hillside with a shrunken stomach. Finally, after more than one hour drive, we

saw a faraway village. We got to it and found out that also there the locals could not show on the map where we were. Apparently, they had never seen a map before.

A short drive further we found a second village and thought that we now knew where we were. Then, all of a sudden we were in the middle of a sandstorm and the road became so

bad that Steffen again thought of turning around. But we could not see a thing and didn't dare to stop, afraid that some truck coming behind us may drive full power into Fuchur. It was a horrible situation, we drove on practically blind and hopping

there was no oncoming traffic, because we didn't know at which side of the road we were. Until the sandstorm died out, we drove in the constant fear of getting off the road. After twenty endless minutes the sandstorm was finally over and through the haze, we saw an asphalt road that had been hidden by the storm. Civilization had us back!

It was getting dark fast now and we had to find a place to spend the night. We found it in front of the Military Museum in Mareth. Next morning, in the museum, a German speaking  guide explained in detail that exactly in this place, during the Second World War, the British and German troops had gotten at each other's throats in a big way, the Germans directly under General Rommel's command. In fact, we could see the bunkers with their connecting tunnels and so vividly visualize how it must have been in those days. It was indeed an adequate final to this off the beaten track adventure in Tunisia.

The Fable of

The Dromedary, the Palm Tree and the Snake

Around noon, when another Sahara Desert day had reached its hottest period, a Dromedary was enjoying a nap in the shade of an imposing Palm Tree, at the fringes of a small oasis. Suddenly he was rudely awakened by an arrogant voice demanding:

— *Get out of my shade, you tramp! I am an important personality in these parts, and you are spoiling my image with your…disheveled looks!*

The Dromedary looked around surprised and annoyed, to find out that the voice belonged to the Palm Tree. He was not young anymore and had gathered a lot of experience in his life. He had seen much of the world, transporting dried dates, palm oil and other fine stuff to India and China, bringing back silk, porcelain, spices and more, for delivery even as far as the shores of the Atlantic Ocean. He was mature enough to be able to control his temper and to handle any kind of person. Irony was one of his psychological weapons and so he replied, still a little sleepy:

— *I am sorry to have upset your majesty so terribly and humbly ask for your forgiveness. But I am a poor, hardworking Dromedary and feel that I deserve some respite … and respect! Your bloody shade is perfect for me and there is no way you can force me out of it.*

— *Oh! A wisecrack this tramp!* Said the Tree and continued: *Listen, I am not only big and beautiful, I am also the producer of the dates from which all the richness of this land flows. Without me you, your employers and finally all the folks in a big part of the world would fall into utter misery. Many would certainly die of hunger!*

The Dromedary was now fully awake and aware of the fact that this discussion would demand more attention than he had expected. After a little thought he answered:

*— Your greatness and beautifulness will excuse me for pointing out that if this here not so good looking traveler didn't take your dates to be sold in distant countries and didn't bring back valuable goods to be sold around here, your dammed dates would not be worth a s**** (Dromedaries— like most people living a hard, adventurous life—sometimes enjoy the use of shocking words). *They would dry out under the desert sun for just nothing at all! At all!*

In this moment a new, sleepy voice–this time a high one–was heard coming out from around the roots of the Palm Tree:

— Can't you guys be quiet? What the hell is this all about? You woke me up and you know that I have to work hard at night! Don't you ever think of others, only of yourselves?

It was the Snake, who lived in her underground home among the Palm Tree roots. Both, Dromedary and Palm Tree, looked at her in surprise. The Dromedary immediately excused himself, honestly regretting having woken her up. The Palm Tree however, in his usual arrogance and already extremely irritated by the Dromedary, spewed his verbal poison (the actual poison being, as everybody knows, the Snake's specialty*):*

- *You disgusting, slippery creature that lives under the protection of my roots, FREE OF CHARGE, what do you want? Just go back to your lousy hole!*

- *You lonesome, conceited and silly old tree*, said the Snake, *you can't just talk like most people do, can you? You always have to insult everybody.*

- *Well said, Snake*, said the Dromedary

- The Palm Tree was now furious: *The purest envy speaks out of you two! You just can't get over the fact that you totally depend on me for your survival*

In the meantime, the Snake had overcome her sleepiness and finally entered full power into the discussion:

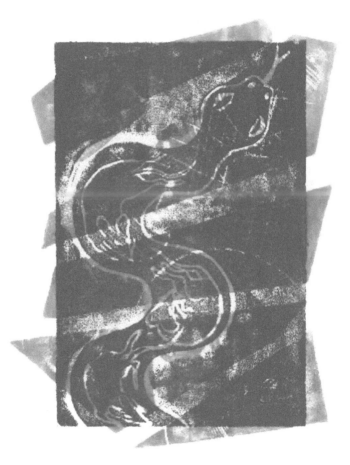

- *Now you indeed overstepped a red line, Palm Tree! The Dromedary has already made very clear the value of his contribution to the world, but you just don't want to understand. Maybe my story will manage to break through to your dumb self...*

- *...I don't care to hear it*, said the Palm Tree.

- *But you will*, retorted the Snake. *I know my job is neither glamorous nor sexy, but without me and my pals keeping the size of the desert rats' and several other hungry populations' under control, they would soon eat up your ah so wonderful fruits and destroy your roots, that I protect as they protect me. You would die a slow and painful death. I may look strange sliding around with no legs, but in all modesty, even you should be able to appreciate the elegance with which I do so. Besides, I am a skilled hunter and the best ranger for this marvelous desert!*

– *Again very well said, Snake,* spoke the Dromedary.

The Palm Tree kept quiet, nobody knew what he was thinking, but the absence of a new outburst of insults made room for some hope that what the Dromedary and the Snake had said was at least starting to interfere with his usual egoistic thoughts. The Dromedary started to get up, saying:

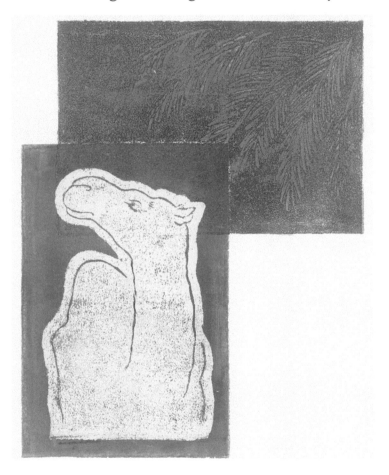

– *I guess all that matters was said and now I have to go. As opposed to our arrogant partner Palm Tree, I was not born into a rich family, blessed with an inexhaustible source of treasured fruits at my disposal. I am an employee and my boss can be pretty nasty if I come too late. But just before I go, let me say this: We all have a function in life, we are all here for a reason and the world needs us all to be able to function, actually to exist. No job is better or more important than any other and we should all respect each other's work. And treat each other accordingly. In this spirit I thank you Palm Tree, for the nice shade.*

And so, the Dromedary trotted off to his employer, while the Snake moved back to her underground cave hoping for some sleep before another busy hunting night. It is not known what the Palm Tree finally made out of what he had heard during this remarkable meeting, but let's be optimistic and hope that he improved on his views and manners.

Malawi Lake

Coming from Mozambique we passed the border into Malawi without a visa. Apparently, there was some squabbling between Malawi and Switzerland over Malawi money in Swiss bank accounts. Anyway, they let us through to fight it out in Blantyre. There we finally got our visas, after explaining to the officer in charge, who accused the Swiss Banks of sheltering the fortunes of corrupt African politicians, how consequently Switzerland dealt with foreign money from criminal provenance. We were very disappointed that the Swiss Ministry of Foreign Affairs never thanked us for that helpfull intervention…

In fact, we were then not at all interested in diplomatic issues, because the Soccer World Cup 2006 was nearing its finals and nothing else was really worth our attention. In Mozambique and now in Malawi we hardly missed a World Cup game, most of which we could watch in our own TV. More of this later.

Since Malawi is generally not so well known I will first highlight the key aspects of its interesting history and geography. Malawi is a very new state, which became independent only in 1964. Before it was the British protectorate of Nyasaland, between 1953 and 1964 as part of a federation with North Rhodesia (now Zambia) and South Rhodesia (now Zimbabwe). Originally, the area was inhabited by several Bantu tribes, which were joined in the early 19th century by invaders from the Yao and Zulu peoples, followed in the 2nd half of that century first by European missionaries and then by European settlers.

Slave trade had a centuries long tradition in Africa and the area of today's Malawi became very early a center of that disgraceful activity. As a consequence of the great efforts made by the famous Scottish explorer Dr. David Livingstone, the first European missionaries arrived together with him in 1861, starting the long fight against slavery, which was only definitely eradicated towards the beginning of the 20th century.

At the time of our visit, Malawi had a population of about 12 million on an area of 94,080 square kilometers (36,324 square miles) land and 24,404 square kilometers (9,422 square miles) water, this mostly on the Malawi Lake. For a small country, Malawi offers a vast variety of beautiful landscapes, from parks and natural reserves to highland wilderness areas with impressive mountains and extensive, undulating grass fields. The population was mostly very welcoming and friendly, non-violent, although in the bigger cities robberies were not uncommon. Still, in those days Malawi was safer than most other African countries. English was generally spoken, beside the various local languages. Malawi is a republic, democratically run, struggling with corruption as lamentably the majority of the countries in today's world.

Now, back to our travels.

Comfortably parked in the friendly Blantyre Country Club, we spent a couple of days watching, with excellent TV-reception, four World Cup games. Unfortunately, this brought us incredible suffering when Brazil deservedly lost to France… But instead of drowning it in scotch, we moved on towards the Malawi Lake. We had read that a lake trip with the ship "Ilala" was an absolute must for anybody visiting Malawi. Its captain was also quite famous, as an interesting, charismatic personality and a very dedicated host to his passengers.

The drive from Blantyre to the small village of Monkey Bay, starting point for the weekly tour of the Ilala ship, was a plunge into real today's Africa. The road lead over Malawi's main river, the Shire River, through lively and pleasant localities as well as through lots of very green, varied vegetation. This road was better than the roads we had suffered in Mozambique and so acceptable to us, modest on road matters as we had lately become…

We spent one beautifully romantic night directly by the Shire River, in Liwonde, as not paying guests of the Hippo View Lodge's owner, a very nice Indian gentleman. We reciprocated by having a wonderful dinner in his fabulous restaurant, also by the river. The exotic sounds emanating from the hippos and the other habitants of the African night bewitched us and made that night unforgettable. It was great music composed by nature itself in an extremely old continent, where most

probably our very first ancestors treaded the Earth. Up to this day I am always deeply touched when remembering that magic night, so lovely shared with my dear, dear wife.

On the First of July 2006 we arrived in Monkey Bay and our first contact was a very young but promising artist, from whom we bought several works, then and during the days that

followed. Because he was always trying to sell his works in the main place of the village and was thus easy to find, he also became something like our local guide. First things first, we soon found out that we had no TV reception in Monkey Bay and the only way to continue to watch the World Cup soccer games would be by joining the local fans in a certain lodge equipped with satellite TV. So, our new artist friend guided us there. After some negotiations with the owner, a South African guy, we could stay there for about USD 5 per night, including water and power, instead of the USD 10 he originally wanted. We

even got one night free of charge! We got a very quiet place in the backyard of the lodge, under huge trees. In the evening, sitting in front of a big TV screen in a fully occupied big room, we watched a soccer game between Germany and Italy, won by the later. We were the only non-Africans in there and Marianne was positively shocked by the massive support the Africans were giving Italy. She asked her left neighbor why they hated Germany so much and he explained that it had nothing to do with hate: it was a purely financial issue, he said.

They had all heavily bet on an Italian victory! Besides, he said, since all African teams were already out, they had agreed to cheer for the French team because it had the biggest contingent of African players…

The next day our artist friend guided us to the so called Ilala Village, the Malawi Lake Services seat, with offices, harbor and shipyard. It was run by a lovely South African couple, Anton and Carolyn. We told them that we wanted to go with the Ilala ship to the Likoma Isle, stay there until the ship's return from the weekly round trip of about 1,000 km (620 miles) and then come back with her to Monkey Bay. They thought it a good plan and Carolyn made our hotel reservations at the island. We were to take our scooter "Moby Dick" with us, leaving Fuchur inside the shipyard during our absence, directly in front of the fulltime occupied security booth, at the entrance. As for the ship's cabin reservation we were to wait for next day's arrival of the Ilala and settle it with the captain himself.

So, the following afternoon, punctually at 2 pm the Ilala docked at its harbor. Anton introduced us to the captain and to the chief steward. We were very disappointed to find out that the famous captain we were expecting, then already an elder gentleman, was sick and his momentarily replacement was his exact opposite; introvert, not communicative at all. But the chief steward, from Zimbabwe, made a very competent and dedicated impression and was indeed later to become a good friend. He showed us around the ship, which was by far not the standard we had expected, but anyway acceptable. However, the only cabins with a bath/WC included were the captain's and the owner's. We went back to Anton and made clear that we wouldn't take any other but the owner's cabin and were willing to pay the price. Fortunately, that cabin was available for our trip. We paid the fare and on 07/07/2006, boarded the famous Ilala.

Before we left, our young artist friend offered us an already almost finished wall clock, carved in wood as a map of Malawi. He intended to finish it until our return from the lake tour. We had to tell him that, sadly, it was too big for us to take back to Switzerland and he was very disappointed. Naturally, none of us could have then known the curious destiny awaiting that clock…

Over a convenient access ramp, Moby Dick could be easily shoved on board the Ilala and parked it in a place that seemed to me to be a quiet one. That place had the additional advantage of being perfectly visible from our cabin. And so, we could see

soon enough how wrong my assumption of quietness had been. On the contrary, Moby Dick was exactly where men, alone on a short trip, liked to gather, near the access ramp! We got very worried and started to search for a better place, a difficult task. However, we noticed that the men were surely curious about our scooter, looked at it and talked about it, but indeed never even touched it. We then decided to leave Moby Dick just where it was, which later proved to be the right thing to do.

Our cabin turned out to be compact but comfortable, the bath/WC not too small and very practical. Anyway, we mostly sat on deck, often right in front of our door and enjoyed the diversified landscape as well as the fascinating activities going on at the many locations where the Ilala anchored. It was all very exotic and also extremely likeable. We were getting more and more addicted to that lazy, very enjoyable

lifestyle and even hardly found the time to read! Our meals we took in the little board restaurant. They were very unusual for us, but interesting and quite tasty.

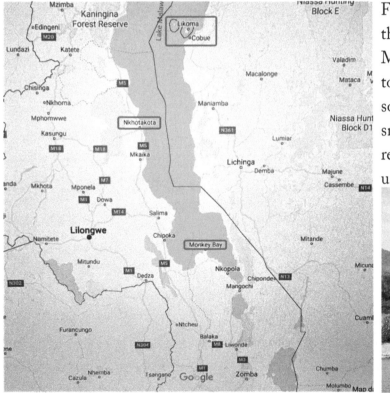

From Monkey Bay to Likoma Island the Ilala cruised the South of the Malawi Lake, were Malawi's main touristic resorts are located, offering all sorts of attractions, like f. i. swimming, snorkeling, diving, kayaking or just relaxing on the beaches, in hotels or under reed huts. We stopped at several

resorts and villages around the lake, including a couple in Mozambique. This gave us a first glimpse of the Ilala's significance as the main connection between these locations.

As the several touristic resorts drifted before our eyes, Marianne and I couldn't help but to think about the strong warning we had shortly read in the Lonely Planet's book about the bilharzia danger. Bilharzia, also called schistosomiasis, is a very dangerous disease if not treated in time. It is otherwise curable but has a long incubation time that sometimes demands several successive tests until it's securely diagnosed. It is transmitted through the skin by little worms carried by water snails (or eventually humans). Therefore, all Malawi Lake's shallow waters, where the snails live, are potential sources of bilharzia transmition. We had decided not to risk a contamination and to be especially careful in Likoma Island.

We had read that Likoma Island was a picturesque place, with some nice beaches, panoramic walks, traditional fishing villages, an imposing cathedral, and–last but not least–very nice local people. Ideal for a few days vacation. By the way, Likoma Island belongs to Malawi, together with its neighbor Chizumulu Island, in spite of both laying at Mozambique's side of the lake border. We thought it would be practical to have our scooter there, to move around easily. Carolyn had told us that at arrival somebody from the hotel would be waiting for us with a car, to show the way from the ship to the hotel. And, crucial, the hotel had a power generator and satellite antenna, so that watching the final World Cup soccer game should be guaranteed! However, as so often, things were not to unfold as expected.

The Ilala let her anker go at Likoma Island around 10 pm of a dark night, inexcusably too late for the World Cup final! The lake was very rough, "choppy lake" the locals call it. The transportation of people and goods between ship and island, quite a considerable distance, could only be carried out by means of the small boats that belonged to the ship. At the island's beach, merchandise was hauled from and to the boats by hand, through the water. For persons, the boats docked against a swimming pontoon anchored near the beach. Between the pontoon and the beach, one had to walk through the water. Naturally, the ship had to be first unloaded of passengers and cargo, before the new cargo and passengers could be brought on board. Already before our ship arrived, people waiting to embark had completely filled up the pontoon, so that those disembarking could hardly walk from the boats to the ladders at the beach facing side of the pontoon.

As Marianne and I boarded the overcrowded pontoon, we immediately started to take stock of the situation and soon found out that:

- We didn't want to wade through the, most probably, bilharzia infested water. And to wade once again, when leaving the island.
- We saw some pick-ups waiting on the beach, but no car from a hotel, which was confirmed by a nice young British couple, brother and sister, waiting on the beach to board. They told us that the only hotel's car had broken down and so, nobody was coming to meet us.
- Moby Dick, with its 160 kg (353 Lbs.) weight, would have to be pushed through the water twice (again on departure). A horror scenario.
- The prospect of more days lazing around on board the Ilala was really, really extremely attractive…

Under these circumstances we decided to forget Likoma Island (remember, we had already missed the soccer final!) and return to the ship, hoping that the owner's cabin would still be free for the rest if the roundtrip. The British brother mentioned above was kind enough to run to the next boat arriving from the ship with cargo, to ask the sailors to make sure that Moby Dick would not be brought to the island.

We had to wait on the pontoon for the last disembarking persons to arrive but managed to get to the Ilala in the first boat returning with boarding passengers. There, we run to "our" cabin which we found closed. We threw our luggage in front of the door, Marianne shoved a chair after it and sat down, swearing that nobody would get into that cabin except ourselves. I run away looking for our friend, the Zimbabwe chief steward, whom I soon found in spite of the crowd milling around all over the deck. After my short but hearty explanation, he just said, *"follow me!"* and went to a very well-dressed man, wearing a suit and a tie, apparently a rich and important person in that area. But evidently this didn't impress the chief steward, who bluntly told him:

- *You can't have the cabin. This gentleman decided to stay on board!*
- *Well,* said the man, *we can surely share the cabin.*
- *No way* replied the chief steward, *he has his wife with him!*

Then he just turned around, told me *"come!"* and in no time opened the cabin door and handed us the keys. The cabin was exactly as we had left it a few hours ago, not even the bed sheets had ben removed. I ran to the window and saw beloved Moby Dick in its usual place: Our new young British friend's intervention had been effective!

After performing something similar to a short Apache dance, followed by several hugs and kisses, we went for a drink, to properly toast the happy end of a remarkable adventure, as well as the continuation of a great holyday. Tourists coming back from Likoma Island told us that the hotel there had no bath and the only bathing possibility was in the lake. They were also all quite disappointed with the tourist attractions of the island that didn't match the advertisements. Further, the locals were said to be unfriendly, something that I can understand when such a small island is overrun by so many tourists. The very worst we heard, however, was that they weren't able to watch the final game of the World Cup, because the power had been disconnected just before the game started… This piece of news helped us to overcome the only regret we had in connection with this adventure.

The days that followed were, as expected, an extension of the ones along the South part of the lake, but much enhanced by the fact that the North part had no tourist resorts, only picturesque native villages from different cultures, each with its own character. Here the importance of the Ilala as

the sole regular connection between the villages and between these and the rest of the world could be fully appreciated. Most of those villages didn't offer docking facilities for the Ilala. But the ship mostly threw her anker close enough for us, just sitting on deck, in front of our cabin door, to view the village and the activities going on there.

The stops were always loudly underscored by a lot of hooting, sirens and the ringing of bells. At each stop, some villagers left the ship and others came on board, some to travel somewhere and a few just to sell or buy stuff. All this was very exciting, colorful, with people laughing, talking and carrying or shoving their incredible luggage that sometimes included goats, bicycles, birdcages and so on. We were often contacted by people selling fruits, sweets or another food

specialty from their village. Some of these visitors came only out of curiosity, to talk to somebody, people like us for instance. Once, a man came asking for money to buy school material for his children; he made a good impression, we thought he was sincere and helped him a bit. Those who couldn't use the ship's boats came in their own little boats, generally a dugout canoe. Fascinating!

On board, the villagers made themselves comfortable, spreading out mainly on the lower deck, in the open as well as in the premises. This deck was often overfilled, with lots of people sitting on the floor, all talking and laughing aloud, a colorful, lively, happy crowd. We used to walk around and to conduct some small talk with them fellow travelers. Quite interesting at times.

As already mentioned, during our cruise the substitute captain was not at all communicative, as diametrically opposed to the real captain, then unfortunately sick. The chief engineer Josh, however, became our best friend. He had studied engineering in Blantyre and right after his graduation went to work in the Ilala, which became his "baby". He kept the engine, the engine room and the annexes immaculate, everything working perfectly. Whenever he had the time, he came to talk to us and at every village he tried to get some food specialty for us to taste. From him we also heard about the interesting histories of some Malawi Lake ships.

The "Guendolin", a 340 tons war ship, was built in the UK and assembled in Mangochi, by the lake, in 1899. She was armed with two cannons to discourage slave traders from crossing the lake and to enforce the British interests against the Portuguese in Mozambique and the Germans in Tanzania. Naturally, the Germans followed suit with a gunship of their own, the "Herman von Wissemann". Regardless of the disputes between the two countries, the British and the German captains became good friends and used to meet for a drink and much conversation. When World War I started, the UK captain received order to sink the German ship. He then sailed to where he and the German captain (who knew nothing about the start of the war) had agreed to meet that day, shot the German ship, disabling her, and took his friend with crew prisoners. This opposite of the proverbial British fair play action was the first sea "victory" of the British Navy in WWI and the only known sea battle on the Malawi Lake. In 1940 the "Guendolin" was converted into a passenger ship and scraped a few years later.

The MV Ilala was actually the Ilala II, replacing a former Ilala that had been built in 1875. Due to her importance for the populations around the Malawi Lake and for the tourism in the area, this unconventional ship, operating in an exotic atmosphere, had become a cult object. She appeared on BBC TV shows and even in Malawi stamps. She had been built in Scotland by the Yarrow Shipbuilders, in Scotstoun by Glasgow, in 1949, and was then transported via Mozambique to Chipoka, by the lake, where she was reassembled. She started operating continuously in 1951 and was totally overhauled once, in the nineties. During its maintenance breaks the Ilala was replaced by the MV Mtendere, a younger ship then stored in the shipyard at Monkey Bay, awaiting to be eventually dismantled to have her parts and components sold.

Towards the end of our cruise Marianne and I catched a nasty cold. In Nkhotakota, where the Ilala could dock, we went on land and in a small but good clinic got adequate medicine.

Back in Monkey Bay, on 07/12/2006, we disembarked Moby Dick, fetched Fuchur, both in perfect shape, and took again our place in the backyard of the lodge. Our originally planned departure had to be postponed for two reasons. First, Josh refused to say goodbye on the ship because he wanted by all means to visit us the next day in Fuchur. Second, because the Ilala ha to be serviced, the Mtendere had to replace her for a while and Anton had invited us to be on board the Mtendere during her test run.

Josh arrived punctually to our appointment in Fuchur, all groomed up in an elegant suit and tie, carrying a huge package. We had thought that as a mechanical engineer the object of his visit was to have a good look at Fuchur. But no, beside his interest in Fuchur that good friend had a mission: To bring us a present that, he explained, was 50% his and 50% of the shipyard, meaning Anton and Carolyn. Now, I wonder if you have already guessed what that present was. No? Well, do you remember the clock our young artist friend wanted to sell us, but we thought was too big to transport? That was it. We were very much touched and thanked all donors effusively but were secretly quite worried about how to take it home. Well, in the end we found a way to pack it diagonally in our biggest trunk and to safely take it to Switzerland, where we even found its ideal place in our small apartment (see picture). To this very day it is still working perfectly, a dear reminder of the good friends we left back there, by the Malawi Lake.

Our last afternoon at the Malawi Lake we spent on board the Mtendere with Carolyn, Anton and another couple, their friends. It was the perfect farewell from those wonderful days. We also discovered that the ship had been built in Travemunde, very near to where Marianne had been born and had grown up. On the morning of 07/14/2006 we once again said goodbye to a precious chapter in our lives, leaving behind a bit of our hearts in a beautiful corner of this marvelous planet of ours and departed, heading for Malawi's Capital

Lilongwe. There we spent two days with Pam, a good friend of our daughter Debi, and her husband John. Both were in the diplomatic service, at the US Embassy, and in their beautiful home we enjoyed great American hospitality.

A little tree at Nambucca Heads

This story is very well recounted by Marianne, but before I leave the stage for her, I must hint at some of the events that took place before they culminated in the Nambucca Heads adventure.

Shortly after taking over Fuchur we experienced a very considerable loss of power that, however, soon disappeared. Some time later it happened again. We then had our engine checked at several Mercedes workshops, in Switzerland and Germany, without any success. The loss of power never occurred at the workshops and neither the Mercedes diagnostics program nor the visual checks showed any irregularity. So, we started on our trip with this "Damocles Sword" hanging over our heads, the power failures continuing to happen in Greece, Turkey and Australia. The Mercedes workshops in these countries were also unable to find the cause. In spite of this problem, on July 8, 2002 we reached Nambucca Heads, a peaceful beach resort in Australia's East Coast, not far from the Pacific Highway, overlooking the mouth of the Nambucca River.

And now I say goodbye, go look for a jolly glass of wine and leave you, dear reader, under Marianne's capable care.

Once again, we had spent a night directly by the sea. The place, located at the foot of the steep coast hill, had been recommended by a friendly couple, campers like us.

In the morning Steffen happily shifts in the first gear, then in the second and briskly drives up the steep narrow road to the highway. After a sharp right curve Fuchur suddenly looses power, wheezes for a few more meters and stops. Steffen tries the first gear again and again, without success. On the contrary, because surprisingly the handbrake isn't holding properly, the car rolls slowly backwards, in small steps, away from the roadbed, until all wheels rest on sand. In spite of the recurring attempts to start uphill, always frustrated by the lack of engine power and by the weak handbrake, we continue to roll backwards, stepwise down the hillside. What shall we do? For me to jump out and shove one of our brake shoes behind a rear wheel seems quite useless, maybe even dangerous for me, at Fuchur's weight and now extreme steep angle.

I reason that to reduce our weight the filled up, 250-liter water tank must be emptied. But a drain valve had not been foreseen, the tank can only be drained through two faucets. To reach these in Fuchur's present steep position I have to lay myself on the floor and crawl to them. All of a sudden there is a strong jolt. Fuchur has hit something and now stands still. I jump out through the side-door, Steffen keeps at the wheel and switches on the rear-view camera. We find out that a little tree, the only tree in the whole area, had stopped us! Going around the car to better evaluate its damage, I find myself standing on the edge of a precipice that runs approximately parallel to the car and falls vertically a long way down to the ocean.

The back door is considerably damaged, but Steffen does use that little tree as a break many more times, until he gets Fuchur roughly perpendicular to the road and so, with the little power available drives back onto it. There is not enough space to turn Fuchur in the direction of our overnight parking, so Steffen rolls down backwards through all the curves, until the very end of the parking space. Then, with the greatest start-up speed he can get and in first gear all the way, he manages to climb up to the road on top.

Due to the whole stress we forget to thank the little tree for saving our lives. Even if I had miraculously been able to jump out before Fuchur fell down the precipice, Steffen, sitting at the abyss side, would have been already too late to do the same. God has saved us by averting the catastrophe, letting us roll against the only tree around!!!

Our Fuchur takes us along the Pacific Highway to the nearest Mercedes workshop, but at not more than 80 km (50 miles) per hour. This time at least the ever-returning loss-of-power-mystery can be finally solved: The thin rubber tube connecting the turbo to the motor, through which pressure differences within the motor start or stop the turbo, as necessary, had been cut too short during manufacturing. Thus, under certain conditions it had been almost disconnected at the motor end, when the resulting loss of pressure told the turbo to stop. For some reason until Nambucca Heads the tube did somehow always slide back to an acceptable connection, preventing detection, but now it had for once completely disconnected, which could naturally be seen. The workshop had no replacement for the too short tube, but they could add about ten inches to it and we never had a loss of power again. Steffen thought of taking legal action against Mercedes but once again we preferred a cozy retirement, without lawyers…

By the way, Fuchur's hand break was also correctly readjusted. The damaged backdoor could still be opened and closed, so we waited to have it fixed later.

Yes, this was one of the two most dangerous situations we faced during our twelve years on the road. As Marianne pointed out, God saved us by "letting us roll against the only tree around". You, dear reader, may find me weird for what I'll put now on paper, but I'll risk doing so: I am even not sure that that little tree was there before we needed it. It is quite possible that God has one or two tricks concerning manipulations of the space-time-continuum, which He applies, for instance, when somebody is about to leave the planet before his/her scheduled time has arrived...

*But actually, I am back here to make one last comment. Surely many of you have already asked why we didn't roll down backwards to the parking space **immediately after the loss of power**. This would have avoided all the risks in which we incurred by trying to regain power or reduce weight, thinking only of reaching the top of the hill. We should have already known that there was not even the danger of a collision with a vehicle coming up, because the parking was empty when we left it. Those of you who ask this question are absolutely right and our honest explanation is very simple: we made a tremendous, almost deadly mistake.*

The sudden loss of power and the unexpected bad performance of the hand break took us by surprise. The spot where this happened couldn't have been more problematic. The sense of urgency was overwhelming and prevented us from stopping a minute to think things over. Only after knowing that we were safe and Fuchur was surely secured against the little tree did we take the time to analyse the situation and find the obvious solution.

I like to believe that neither Marianne nor I were/are especially dumb or at all prone to panic, but this experience showed us that under an extreme time constraint we forgot to think a bit and spontaneously followed the wrong course of action. This insight showed us how eminently important is specific emergency training for everybody who deals with potentially dangerous equipment, like pilots for instance, although I doubt that a situation like the one we had been in could ever be foreseen.

* * *

I guess it was normal that we needed some time to get over the Nambucca Heads shock. As we drove on North, along Australia's East Coast, we often talked about it, again feeling in our bones the dread of that day. But human nature being as it is, the time came when our memories started to subside and an increasingly relaxed dealing with this issue developed, until finally a very special day brought us back to our old selves.

After forty-five sunny, quiet but also interesting days in the wake of our meeting with the little tree, we reached the area surrounding the Conway National Park, in Queensland, with the best access to the biggest living organism in our planet: The Great Barrier Reef. Just before reaching the locality of Proserpine, in the morning of 08/13/2002, we saw at the left side of the road the usual tourist information center, typically to be found when one approaches Australian townships. We stopped there and were attended by an extremely nice and efficient lady, Simone, who had great tips in stock for our next days. One tip was a quad drive, another one was fish observation from a special boat equipped with underwater windows, then there were ship tours to the beautiful islands of the Whitsunday Group and last but not least, the best tip of all: A very special visit to the Great Barrier Reef, for which we had to wait four days.

In the morning of 08/17/2008 we locked up Fuchur, left it in the parking space where we had spent the night and walked over to the helicopter base, from where we started our flight to the Great Barrier Reef, about 65 km (40 miles) away. Peter, the pilot, had been expecting another passenger who didn't come, so he started right on time without him or her. However, five minutes later he was called back in order to fetch said passenger, who had finally arrived. To our big surprise the delayed passenger was the Simone from the tourist office, who was a friend of Peter and had decided to join Marianne and me for the flight!

According to plan, the flight was interrupted at the Whitsunday Island, where we landed on the famous Whitehaven Beach, considered by many the longest and finest beach in Australia. After a glass of excellent champagne, we proceeded to the Great Barrier Reef, admiring on the way some beautiful islands and reefs, including the reef containing what Marianne and I called "The Lonely Heart of Nature".

Our objective was an observation platform consisting of two pontoons floating above the

Reef. One pontoon was very simple, just a landing surface for helicopters. The other, a bigger one, offered not only a wharf for the tourist ships but also

a comfortable infrastructure for visitors, including a canteen, toilets and observation facilities. After landing we were taken to the bigger pontoon in a rubber boat

and there served a generous cold meal.

After that Peter flew the helicopter back to the coast. Simone went with him. We were shown the Reef, first through the underwater windows of the pontoon and afterwards from a boat with a glass bottom. Some other visitors were swimming around with snorkels or were even really diving in proper diving suits and with oxygen tanks. The area they were allowed to access was strictly limited, to protect the Reef.

We were disappointed by the lack of colors on the Reef itself and on the fish swimming around, which by the way were not as numerous as we had expected. We were then told that the colors could only be brought out when photographing or filming with special illumination and filters, an explanation that left us extremely skeptic… Months later in Western Australia, when snorkeling above the Ningaloo Reef, we saw all those spectacular colors with just our naked eyes. Much later we found out that the reason for the absence of colors I mentioned above was the slowly dying of the Reef, primarily as a consequence of human activities, in that specific place mainly the tourism. We had witnessed the beginnings of the problems that were to become life-threatening for the Great Barrier Reef and in those days were still being pushed aside even by some people who should have known better.

In spite of us missing the Reef colors, that day was just superb, opening our eyes once again to the bright side of life and showing Nambucca Heads in the right perspective: as an incident, gratefully without any serious consequences. The day was crowned by a return to the mainland (some ill-intentioned people, **absolutely not like me** but like most New Zealanders, would say "return to the **big island**"...) on board of a small ship, sailing along the enchanting island world of the Whitsunday Group. A great dinner in a small, cozy beach restaurant up-rounded it all.

The Blooming Desert

Marianne, the great planer and organizer, found out at the very beginning of our Southern Africa exploration, that in Namaqualand, a plateau on South Africa's Northwest, Northern Cape Province, a most remarkable yearly phenomenon was going to take place: The Blooming Desert. She immediately determined that we must under no circumstance miss it. Therefore, she made sure that we timed our first of two planned Southern Africa round trips so as to arrive at Namaqualand not later than the middle of August, because said temporary phenomenon always happens between that date and the middle of September.

Namaqualand is limited at the North by the border to Namibia and at the West by narrow, sandy, rather unattractive Atlantic Ocean beaches. To the East it mingles with the dry planes known as "Bushmanland", which eventually merge into the desert at the South of the Kalahari Region, in Botswana. Both Namaqualand and the Southern Kalahari are often described as "desert-like", but do believe me, this is highly understated: They are mostly real deserts by Marianne's and my standards… Leaving Namaqualand towards the South, entering the Western Cape Province in the direction of Cape Town, vegetation improves and beautiful, world famous flowers thrive there. These flowers, however, cannot match the ones that bloom in the vastness of Namaqualand's Desert, during that yearly short-lived phenomenon dear Marianne so consequently lead us to meet!

The rough frontier town of Springbok considers itself the capital of Namaqualand. It is the busy service center for the surrounding copper and diamond mines and lies in the middle of the blooming flowers when they explode in August-September.

As hinted above, we rounded Southern Africa twice. Both times we entered Namaqualand from Namibia. The first time we arrived in Namibia with plenty of time to explore that interesting country, while keeping ourselves informed about the flower situation in Namaqualand. So, before passing the South African border we not only visited Namibia's generally known sites of interest, but also visited a San and a Himba villages, each fascinating in its own, very special way and both receiving us with great hospitality. Deals were also locally closed, as shown here...

CLOSING A DEAL...

The San **The Himba**

When we found out that the Namaqua flowers were starting to bloom, we drove to them. But nothing we had read or heard prepared us for what we found there.

Flowers do bloom in many deserts of this planet of ours, but seldom, if at all, with the magnificence observed in Namaqualand. And, which is more, never with that specific "Swiss watch" regularity, which is a consequence of the regularity of the local rains. It is true that not all Namaqualand bloomings are the same, but they are all extraordinary. We were extremely lucky, the locals told us, because the 2006 one was being considered the best in the last twenty years! I am convinced that's due only to Marianne's so enthusiastic expectations and efforts not to miss it, bless her.

When we reached the flowers, they were already at their zenith and if I try a thousand years,

I'll never be able to justly describe what we experienced. Maybe Goethe could do it. Not even any picture of that event that I have ever seen fully conveys our impressions. In no picture are the colors as brilliant as in reality. Further, the smells are naturally missing in them, the sounds as well; there is no buzzing of the thousands of busy insects.

And—last but not least—no picture can convey that overwhelming feeling of being yourself inside a huge painting, made of all possible and impossible colors, extending beyond the horizon... I have, however, no other choice but to show here a few pictures, to at least try to give you, dear reader, a rough idea of what it was like.

To properly visualize the unbelievable botanical wealth of Namaqualand, it is helpful to

remember that we are looking at a variety of not less than 4,000 plant species. During the very long dry season, corresponding to the whole year

except for the few blooming weeks, many thousands of seeds survive in each square yard,

in wait of the liberating rainfall in August and September. As shown in the pictures, the different species are sometimes closely mixed up, but can also build larger areas occupied only by a locally dominant species. This results in an infinite number of amazingly

different color combinations.

In Namaqualand we also discovered a new kind of physical condition: Drunkenness from the consume of colors. After a certain number of hours in that hyper colored world, we felt as drunk as if we had had several glasses of wine. We even remained in this state for long hours after we finally, two days later, had left Namaqualand!

At the end of our second Southern African round trip we again visited Namaqualand, this time during Christmas and found a desert. A bleak landscape, as you can see by comparing the two pictures bellow, taken from exactly the same point.

<table>
<tr><td>August 30, 2006</td><td>December 25, 2006</td></tr>
</table>

But we must be positive and consider that also the desert has a beauty of its own. For Marianne and me, however, the Blooming Namaqualand remained a strong candidate for the title of SUPREME HIGHLIGHT of all our travels.

Before closing this story, I must tell about a very touching side-happening that took place when we moved from Namibia into South Africa during our second round trip. The Namibian border office was a small house in which a clerk for the passport control and another one, a lady, for the customs issues, sat together. When checking my passport, the clerk noticed that it was my birthday and in a very kind gesture stood up for congratulations and a handshake. The customs lady saw this and came forward to sing to me a birthday song in her native language, followed by a hearty hug. So, you don't have to ask why Marianne and I loved Africa so much! It was not only the blooming desert alone.

A Day To Forget

It was still dark when in October 17 of the year 2008 we landed in Buenos Aires, once again returning from our yearly sojourn in Switzerland. A talkative but very friendly cab driver delivered us and our considerable luggage to the Club Alemán de Gimnasia, in the district of Lomas de Zamora. After the long flight we were happy to be back to our Fuchur and to the wide green area of the club, with its big trees and sport fields, not to mention the nice people. As in the former years, Fuchur had been well cared for during our absence. We found everything as we had left. After a good shower, a hearty welcome from our great friends, the club property administrators Laura and Pocho, as well as some unpacking and reinstallation, we took a well-deserved nap, followed by a generally lazy, cozy day.

Next morning, the old spirit properly restored, we energetically set out to get the car ready for the new adventures we had in mind. While at work, we were spotted by an Argentinian gentleman (by then the club was only in name "Alemán", German,) walking past. We knew him only by sight but with the typical Argentinian hospitality he came to say hello and to welcome us back. We started to chat and when he heard that we were heading for Paraguay his expression took a very worried look. He said:

Ohooo! You will have to drive through Entre Rios… That province has the most corrupt police of Argentina, a shame to our country! And they are especially keen on mugging foreigners. Once they stopped an elderly German couple I know and extorted 800 USD from them, for "faulty" things they "identified" in their motorhome, that were absolutely legal in this country. But don't worry, I have something to help you guys. I'll be back in a moment.

He returned with a form from the Argentinian Ministry of Foreign Affairs that should be completed by a police officer when applying a fine. The policeman or policewoman had to fill in his/her name, grade, number, amount fined and the corresponding justification, as well as the personalia of the individual fined. Further, a picture of the police officer must be glued in as well. Our friend assured us that this document was authentic, official, primarily for the use of the people employed by that ministry. I immediately made several good quality copies of it and started to think how best to present and explain it to a police officer, hopping that this would never become necessary…

Two days later we left the club and after some good time spent in Buenos Aires and surroundings, we drove Northwest to Rosario and then North, along the Paraná River, towards Paraguay. From Santa Fe we crossed the River to reach Paraná, the capital city of the Province Entre Rios (meaning "between the Rivers" Paraná and Paraguay). From Paraná we intended to continue North between the two rivers mentioned, along Road 127, so as to visit the Argentinian National Park of Iberá before crossing the border into Paraguay.

Well, when entering the city of Paraná, the first event happened which would make December 4, 2008, a day to forget (in addition to the economic crisis, that made the whole 2008 a year to forget…).

The road we were on was a reasonably wide highway with two lanes in each direction and a metal plank in the middle. I was driving, Marianne was navigating. Traffic was normal, the road not too crowded. Suddenly there was a tremendous noise not far away behind us. I had a look at the mirror and saw an old automobile stuck against the metal plank, while parts were still flying around and settling down on both sides of the highway. I commented that we had been lucky, since all happened away enough from us for any flying part to hit Fuchur. Marianne suggested that we stop to help, but I replied that not being locals we could hardly be of real use. Besides, I had seen that several cars were already stopping when I looked at the mirror. She agreed.

A red light stopped us one or two miles later. While we waited for the green light, a small motorbike stopped at Marianne's side and a young man, clad only in shorts, jumped down from it. He hung himself from our side mirror and started to scream confused stuff through the closed window. My Spanish is quite good, but I couldn't understand what he was trying to say. Marianne cranked down the window, but it didn't really help. She then did something amazing: she spoke, let's say, very energetically, to him … in German! Surprisingly, this really worked. He calmed down and started to speak quite normally, explaining he was the driver of the accident car and that we had pushed him out of the road and forced him to hit the plank. It was pure nonsense and Marianne wanted to ignore it, but I thought this might give the impression that we were fleeing because we felt guilty and so attract the unwelcome attention of Argentinian justice. We therefore decided to turn around and go back to the "scene of the crime" for clarification. We invited the now calmer driver into Fuchur and took him back with us. During the whole following short drive, he kept trying to convince us of our "guilt".

I started to think of our friend at the Lomas de Zamora club but in spite of his warnings concerning the Entre Rios police, I still thought that even in Entre Rios the police would be necessary and demanded its presence. For the insurance company at least, we could not have avoided it.

Arriving at the accident site we found out that the driver had not been alone in the car: an even younger guy had also been there, who was now looking extremely disturbed, even guilty. Considering that "loss of control of the vehicle" had evidently been the cause of the accident, Marianne and I immediately and independently from each other thought that probably this youth had been the one really at the wheel, without a driving license and being instructed by the older guy, now posing as the driver. Shifting

the cause of the accident to me would not only solve their financial problem of repairing or replacing their car but would naturally also improve their stand before the judge. So would switching the drivers. No wonder the desperate effort being made by the guy who had followed us in shorts, on the backseat of a friend's motorbike! However, we couldn't prove any of this. We also wondered to whom the heavily damaged vehicle really belonged.

The police, two young policemen, arrived at approximately the same time as we did. Somebody had evidently already

called them. First, they heard the "driver's" story. Then I explained that I had never been on the left lane, that I had sometimes deviated away from the right edge of the road

due to the many "potholes" there but had not gone over the left separation line. I then pointed out that none of the parts that had been flying around and were still lying about had hit Fuchur, which would have been impossible if we had indeed been in a position to force the other car out of the road. Unfortunately, there were no witnesses: all who had seen the accident had disappeared (for good reasons, I'm sure…).

Regardless of the obvious facts, the two policemen took the side of the "driver" and started a game of "Good Cop" and "Bad Cop". It was clear that they thought us very rich and, if properly "motivated", willing to pay instead of going through a lot of trouble. And if we paid, the police would certainly take the lion's share.

We kept talking to these cops, trying to show how absurd it was to try to involve us in the accident. Marianne could be very convincing. She spoke no Spanish but understood it well and she spoke a very clear, easy to follow Portuguese, so that she could communicate with the locals. I showed the cops our insurance documents which made clear that I was not allowed to negotiate any deals, even less to make concessions and that I had to leave all negotiations to the insurance company lawyers.

In the face of such a fierce opposition the policemen somehow expected support from the technical police team and summoned them. We were very surprised when this team arrived: a professional bunch, lead by an elderly, very experienced, no-nonsense lady. They took measurements and pictures, filled forms and were finished in no time. Then the lady asked for the other car involved. Bad Cop told her not to bother, that car had not been at all damaged. He should have kept quiet. All hell broke loose: she rubbed him all over the ground, asking were he had gotten his police training, if any, why he had summoned her team when it was clear that the second vehicle–being undamaged–could not possibly be involved in the accident and so on. Actually, she explained our arguments again but in a much more effective, colorful way. After this awesome outburst, she and her team disappeared in a cloud of dust.

Marianne and I were understandably highly amused. We were starting to go say goodbye but there were apparently very big expectations on our financial resources and a last effort was made by Good Cop. We had to admire his resilience. He came to us and asked me aside. He said:

— *You know, even if you are not responsible for this accident, it will still take several days to get the paperwork done. It's a lot of bureaucracy, very disagreeable and you will have to stay here in Paraná all the time. Why don't you give those poor guys 5'000 Dollars to fix their old car, that's nothing for you, and go enjoy your travels?*

— *I am sorry*, I said, *but I am leaving very soon. I just have to call the insurance company and hand this case over to them. Then one of their lawyers will come talk to you and you can explain whatever you like to him. And by the way, to me 5'000 Dollars is a hell of a lot of money.*

After this dialogue Good Cop disappeared, never to be seen by us again. Bad Cop, however, came over in a reserved but not unfriendly mood, asking us to come to the police station to sign the protocol, before we left. We needed a copy for the insurance company anyway. In the police station we had a long wait. First Bad Cop had to write down the dammed protocol and after that we had to send it back four times for corrections, before I could sign it. Surprisingly, all mistakes were to our great disadvantage…

A last remark of interest: This whole incident cost us a total of 3,5 hours.

We were glad to leave Paraná behind but at the same time a little proud of having satisfactorily handled that challenge. Northeast of the city we encountered Road 127 which we followed along a very empty stretch. No villages, not even houses and few vehicles on the road. We saw a Gaucho in the typical attire, with two beautiful horses. We greeted each other and stopped for a little chat. He told us that he was taking those hoses to a big "fiesta" (festivity) and invited us to come along and enjoy the event too. Without knowing what was still coming our way, we thought we had had enough "fiesta" for that day, thanked him, wished him a great time and preceded on route.

Some miles later we saw to our right a small brick house, still under construction, in front of which was parked a police car. Close by the road stood three policemen, one of which moved to stop us. He proved later to be the boss of the other two. Since no other vehicle had been stopped by these cops, we immediately assumed that they had been hounded against us by their colleagues from Paraná, which was practically confirmed during the proceedings that followed. I was ordered out of Fuchur, Marianne could remain inside and immediately started, as discreetly as possible, to film and to take pictures, documenting the proceedings. After seeing my papers, which the boss kept, they took me around the car, showing all its "wrong" features. I was being treated like a criminal, but still rebuffed all their absurd accusations, of which I give some examples:

- The "Bullgrid" in front was allegedly illegal in Argentina.
- So were the trailer rack and the step for entering the car (integral part of the vehicle delivery) in the back.
- An indication of the maximal vehicle speed was missing in the back (we were no truck).
- No fluorescent markings on the sides.

And so on.

When we had been all around Fuchur I positioned myself so that by looking at me they were looking away from Fuchur. This because one of the cops had earlier noticed Marianne filming and had become quite angry. For a moment I had been afraid that he was going to enter the car and snatch the camera, but Marianne flashed a bewitching smile at him and made signs that she was putting that camera away, which had calmed him down. I suppose that it probably also occurred to him that she at least couldn't record the voices from inside the car. Anyway, Marianne being Marianne had naturally continued filming and I for sure didn't want them to notice it.

I pointed out that upon our arrival in Argentina, before we were allowed to leave the harbor, the Buenos Aires police had thoroughly checked the car and had found no faults. Further, we had already driven throughout all of Argentina and no police control had found anything wrong with our vehicle. The boss answered that it was not his fault if the others didn't know their jobs. I remarked that it was very sad for Argentina that only the Province of Entre Rios had competent police officers, but my sarcasm went ignored and, after taking a picture of Fuchur, all three of them stood there looking angrily at me.

I waited a bit for them to say something, but they were not forthcoming, so I said:

- *How much is the total fine for all our transgressions? Remember, we only have to drive to the Paraguay border. Tell me the amount and I'll pay it. Oh, but I have to ask you for something, just a moment, please.*

I made a discreet sign to Marianne, to stop filming, went to the car and came back with the document from the Ministry of Foreign Affairs, which I silently handed to the boss. They stuck their heads together to have a look at it. I presume that the big set of words on top, "MINISTRY OF FOREIGN AFFAIRS" was responsible for what followed: A totally unexpected pass of magic. The two subordinate cops simply vanished and, in opposition to the usual development in such magic presentations, never came back! We haven't ever figured out where they went, perhaps another universe. The boss must have been immune to the magic, because he was still standing there, musing. Certainly, about how to handle the new circumstances. He was not very creative, because the best he could manage was the question:

- *Where did you get this?*
- *You know,* I said (I had planed this right after receiving that form in Lomas de Zamora), *as part of my work for the Swiss government, in Bern, I have a lot to do with the Argentine Embassy and have made many friends there. When they heard I was coming here, they gave me this, to be filled by any police officer that fines us. I guess it's for some statistics, but it seems important for them. They especially stressed that the picture of the responsible officer, in this case certainly you, must be glued to the form.*

Now he really had to carefully think this over, for which I had total understanding. After a while he finally talked again:

– *Yeeeees, a have already been thinking that you are our guests and very nice people. And after all, you are leaving the country for good* (his own wishful thinking, I never said it and we did return later, but certainly not through Entre Rios) *in a couple of days. I am ready to close both eyes and let you go without fines, but I have to talk to my boss first.*

I was having difficulty in keeping a straight face and not bursting out in laughter but managed to thank him and say I'd wait for him to make his call. He got out his cellphone and moved away, so I couldn't hear what he was saying. Every time I tried to come near him, he went further away. My guess was that he was calling his brother cops in Paraná to explain the situation. After about five minutes he came back and informed that his boss had agreed.

However, he was not to be stopped from trying to prove to me that all his earlier demands had been absolutely lawful... I was invited to the little brick house, that turned out to be a real police post, in use although not yet finished, where he showed me a "book". It was not printed but made out of Xerox copies, bound to look like an official regulation, even with a regulation number. The content seemed to be put together from copies of parts of some real regulations, combined with texts written specifically to outlaw components and characteristics of the average motorhome. Looking carefully, one could notice the type of the letters changing along the pages. In some places the borders of pieces of paper containing text, that had been glued to the original pages, had been inadvertently copied and could be perceived as faint lines. Those corrupt cops had really prepared themselves as well as they could for their assaults against (in their eyes) rich foreign motorhome travelers. We had been lucky with our friend's document and my Spanish knowledge, but average tourists were very much defenseless.

I made a note of the regulation number written on the "book" and told him that I would try to buy one, so that in the future I would know what was legal in Argentina. He put on a forced smile and said it was a good idea but could not really disguise some worry. My small revenge.

Since he was now posing as my good pal, I told him that it was almost dark and that we needed a place for the night. If there was a gasoline station nearby? He recommended one 6 km North, on the outskirts of a small locality called Sauce de Luna and promised to pass by every hour to make sure all was well with us. We didn't check on that promise because that night we went to sleep very early, tired as we were after that day to forget.

Next morning, we stopped at the locality of Federal, from where I called the insurance company to inform them about the happenings in Paraná. Afterwards I faxed them a short report about it, together with a copy of the police protocol. For good measure we also bought and glued to the back of our van a sign indicating our maximal speed, thus trying to discourage more corrupt cops from stopping us in the hope of finding faults with our car.

The National Park of Iberá was worth our visit and the rest of the drive to Paraguay went smoothly. Before closing this story however, I must add an experience we made in Corrientes, a very likeable city near the border with Paraguay, at the confluence of the rivers Paraná and Paraguay. We were looking around for a place to stay for a couple of days, when two very imposingly uniformed policemen on two beautiful motorbikes approached us and said they had the impression that we were looking for something, if they could help? After our last meetings with the Entre Rios police, this was for us almost unbelievable. We told them what we were looking for and they said that there was a place by the river, covered with trees (it was extremely hot in Corrientes), were we could stay free of charge. It was however at the other end of the city, difficult to explain how to get there and so they would show us the way. And we crossed the whole city of Corrientes escorted by two police motorbikes, as if we were indeed the VIPs from Bern I had suggested to the cops at the Road 127… The place they showed us was all that they had promised and they even took the trouble to tell us how everything worked, which were the best restaurants nearby and so on. When we tried to give them something for a beer or a coffee, they absolutely refused it, saying that they were only doing the job they were already being paid for!

Just by coincidence, the following day we met the boss of those two outstanding policemen. He was the Chief of Police of Corrientes and was personally training a young cop. A fine gentleman of the old school, this Chief of Police took his work extremely seriously and not only chose his people with the utmost care, he also himself proudly passed to them his high moral values and work standards. After meeting him, we realized why Corrientes had such a brilliant police force. We could not help but to think of the stunning contrast to the Entre Rios police. The reason for this was now crystal clear and Marianne brought it to the point by remembering an old saying from the North German fishermen:

THE FISH ALLWAYS STARTS TO STINK FROM ITS HEAD

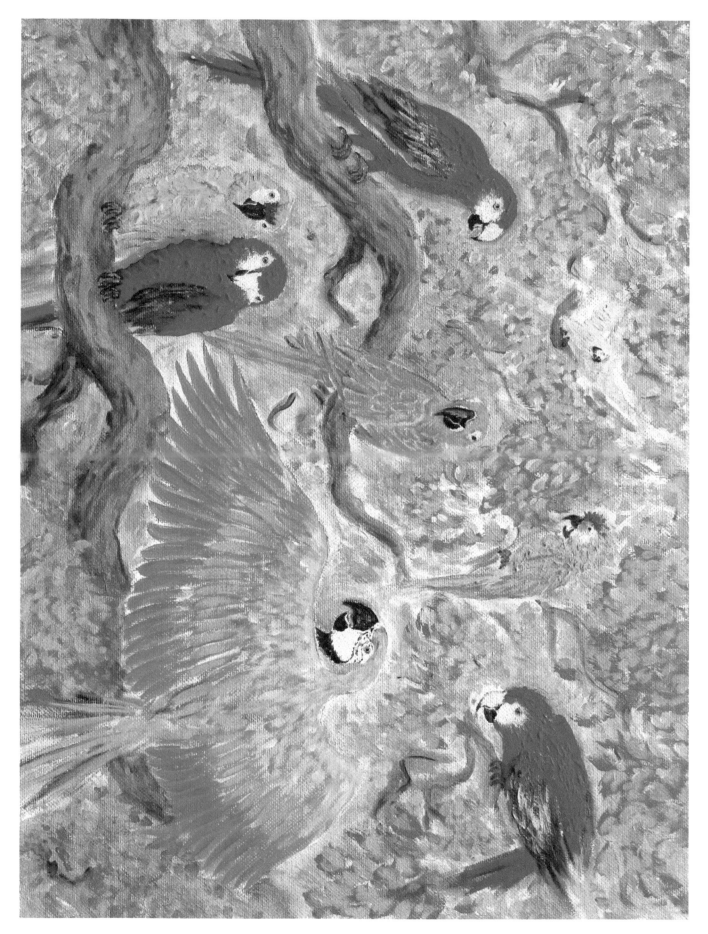

The Fable of

The Aras and the evil in their midst

Every day, in the late afternoon, the Aras used to meet at the luxuriant canopy of the Jacarandá (Brazilian Rosewood) tree, right in front of the vertical stonewall containing their nests, well protected in recesses and small caves, in which their little ones were free from the many predators that threatened them. The Aras were extremely proud of the merrily easygoing, free and democratic spirit that characterized those meetings. There were all possible kinds of Aras participating: red, blue-yellow, green, even a couple of the seldom blue ones. Also, all ages were represented, from the children that still had trouble with their flying to some very old individuals who had trouble flying due to some old age afflictions. Often, guests from other groups were present too, as well as newcomers to the group, all gladly welcomed. Everybody had the same rights and duties. Naturally, sometimes the very young had to be scolded by the older ones. However, as we shall find out next, things had not always been like this.

We all know how lovable, very clever, actively humorous and… loud those birds are. And so were their noisy, jolly colorful late afternoon meetings. A very important personality in those meetings was the Keeper of History, in the present case an elderly Blue-Yellow lady Ara with the characteristic deep knowledge of all Keepers of History. Additionally, she commanded a great wealth in life experience. As a young Ara she had even personally fought in the so-called Great Battle.

To those not familiar with the ways of the Aras, a short explanation: As in all societies without writing, even among the humans, their whole history is memorized by the Keepers of History, highly intelligent individuals with an exceptional memory. The Keepers also have the duty to choose their replacements, to whom they transmit all the knowledge that they themselves had received from their predecessors plus what they had added during their own time. The

Keeper of History is always a Storyteller too, trying by this method to foster the whole group's awareness of their history and also to spread some wisdom among them.

One pleasant afternoon the Aras were surprisingly quiet, enjoying a cool breeze after an extremely hot day, when a teenager Red Ara, already noted in the group for his lively wits and curiosity, addressed the Keeper of History:

- *Mam, I always hear about the* **Great Battle** *and about some very evil Red Aras. What happened? What was it really all about?*
- *Well,* said the Keeper, *it's a long story but I consider it important that the young ones learn all about it.* And addressing the group: *Shall I tell it now?*

The comments went from "by all means" to "oh, not again!", but the majority was for it, either out of curiosity (young ones) or for pedagogic reasons (parents and grandparents). The Keeper decided to tell.

* * *

About fifty years ago we were facing a very difficult time. A sickness had spread among many trees in the forest. As a consequence, almost all the fruits we normally eat were either not forthcoming or had developed a terrible taste. Hunger, anger and despair were rapidly spreading among our people, as well as among all others who depended on fruits for survival. Not even the wisest leaders knew what to do and could only recommend calm and patience.

Under these circumstances, a small but very evil group of Red Aras felt that it was their chance to get to power and affluence. Their ideas were very simple and extremely stupid. Morals, decency and compassion were not included in them, but hate was their compass. In short, they declared a small minority, the Blue Aras, to be responsible for the problem with the trees, saying that they had poisoned them to kill all other Aras and thus become the only Aras to enjoy all food and good places in the forest. The Blue Aras were doing this, the evil ones said, because they were an inferior race, bad to the core and had to be totally destroyed in order not to contaminate the only superior and pure race, the Red Aras. For this same reason, avoidance of racial contamination, all other Ara small minorities had also to be destroyed, as well as the Aras born with defective bodies and minds. Later this murderous madness was extended to the Red Aras who opposed the evil ones, that were declared "traitors to their race".

The evil ones also preached that other races like the Blue-Yellow and the Green Aras, although numerous, were not as dangerous as the mentioned minorities but just inferior races, to be kept apart and "tamed" to serve the red ones.

Now, you may ask how the evil Red Aras could possibly get the other Red Aras to follow these absurd ideas, which I can now tell you, most of them did! You have to remember the situation I already described: Hunger, anger, despair. The evil ones told the other Red Aras that they were a superior race, invincible, and thus capable of taking the scarce edible food away from the other Aras. Also, that with the poisonous Blue Aras liquidated, the food would return. Further, they stressed that as the dominating race, the Red Aras would become the sole masters of everything important: food, the best places in the forest and all other surviving Aras to serve them. The not so clever portion of the Red Aras and those with a weak character were easily lured by these visions. The corrupt ones joined in opportunistically, hoping for some personal profit. The intelligent Red Aras—naturally much less numerous than the rest of them—who saw the absurdity and the danger of the situation, either fled away or tried to fight the evil and were cruelly murdered. A great number, especially those with a family, went along in an effort to avoid trouble. Still, the evil Red Aras were rightly afraid that the insights of the wise ones may spread and open the eyes of the population in general, endangering their new power position. To prevent that, they, who didn't know what compassion is, rapidly added repression through physical violence to the already massive psychological pressure on their followers. After that, ruthless terror soon became integrated in the daily routine of those poor, manipulated Red Aras. With all kinds of benefits, the evil ones bought the loyalty of criminal Aras, even non-red ones, who carried out the violence, barbarous murder included.

Meanwhile what did the non-red Aras do in the face of these developments? Unfortunately, at first, when evil was still weak and easy to fight, nothing. Out of a mixture of laziness, ignorance and cowardice they fell into a mood of wishful thinking and did nothing. Some, incredibly, felt indeed attracted to the evil ideas, completely ignoring that they were directed against themselves as well! Even after the horrible so-called "christal night", when hundreds of Blue Aras were murdered by the hordes of Red Aras contaminated by the evil ideas, when the little Blue children were brutally murdered in front of their parents, before the parents themselves were equally murdered, no real reaction came from the majority of the Aras.

Only a relatively few very brave Aras risked their lives, some even lost theirs, helping the Blue ones—especially the children—to escape or hiding them. By the way, the word "christal" comes from the fact that the evil Aras, out of mockery, "decorated" the empty caves of the murdered Blue Aras with beautiful small christals from the riverbeds, before taking these caves for themselves.

So, the great majority of the Aras saw the huge, dark clouds of the advancing storm gathering at the horizon but chose to declare them a passing shower. As evil, totally unchallenged, continued to spread and could not be ignored any more, the non-Red Aras started to engage the evil Red Aras in appeasement meetings, which only lead to concessions in favor of the arrogant and demanding evil ones. Finally, at the brink of a total domination of the Ara world by the evil ones, the rest of the Aras, including many good Red ones, joined forces and in the terrible Great Battle, with thousands of casualties, dead and for life disabled Aras on both sides, managed to defeat the evil.

As for the problem with the trees, these eventually healed themselves and the good fruits returned in quality and in quantity. This was a lucky turn of events because the evil ones, with their stupid explanation of the food problem as a conspiracy of the Blue Aras, had blocked a serious search for real solutions.

It is clear that none of the leading evil Aras participated in the battle. They kept at a safe distance and let the misguided Red Aras sacrifice themselves in the belief of their duty to "protect the honor and existence of their superior race". The cowardice of the evil ones became evident in the tribunal held by the Council of the Elders, after the Great Battle: those evil ones, formerly so arrogant, so destitute of any form of compassion, were now a wretched bunch of despicable beings, swearing ignorance of all evil, trying to shove responsibility to one another and some committed suicide. Those who didn't were sentenced to death by the tribunal. Actually, their cowardice had been clear from the start, because they only attacked those who couldn't defend themselves, like very old, very young and disabled Aras, or when many evil ones went together against a single good Ara. Typically, the evil ones only directed their hate against tiny, completely outnumbered minorities. The great mass they cowardly flattered, manipulating them towards their evil purposes.

* * *

After a short pause the Keeper of History looked around and asked if there were any questions. The same teenager who had started the conversation asked now:

- *You told us what happened to the evil ones after the Great Battle. But what did happen to their followers and especially to the ones that had really collaborated with the evil ones?*
- *That's precisely the question I was hopping for,* said the Keeper. *You are a clever one, young boy! We must talk later. I still have no successor...*

A murmur came from the public and many admiring looks met the now very embarrassed teenager. The Keeper proceeded:

> — *The real collaborators, the ones who had in fact evilly acted, were whenever possible identified and judged by the Council of the Elders. The murderers and other capital criminals were killed, the less evil, like the corrupts for instance, were punished in other ways, according to their crimes. The followers who had not committed crimes were, let's say, "reeducated". It was at lest tried to make them understand how wrong they had been. And here starts the great problem we now face!*

The Keeper waited a bit for any questions or comments. The Aras, however, kept quiet, anxiously expecting her to continue. Even those who knew something thought that she could indeed best explain things. She then continued her story:

> — *You see, not all of the criminals could be identified or found. Some fled to other parts of the forest and started a new life. Others, that had been less visible, just mingled among us and remained discreetly undercover, so to speak. Further, a number of the followers could not be "reeducated". For a while they concealed this, but secretly continued to cherish the crazy dream of belonging to a superior race. As time went by and the memory of the horrible events started to fade from the heads of the majority of the Aras, those incorrigible followers, as well as many of the escaped criminals, became less cautious and started to try to influence their children and other youngsters towards their own beliefs. These "neo-evil" ones and their new disciples then got together in small groups and, as we all know, are right now trying to regain influence. **The evil is back and must be fought, now,** before it grows again so big that many, many, many must suffer and die!!! And today is a great opportunity for us to talk about it and to think how best to proceed.*

A very old but still strong Green-Ara, a veteran and a hero of the Great Battle, where he had lost his left leg and badly damaged his right wing, raised his famous strong voice:

> — *What you have told now, Keeper, is in fact well known to most of us here and I have already spent a lot of my unfortunately plentiful idle time thinking it over. If you all care to hear, I can deliver a short presentation of my conclusions.*

After signs of general approval, the veteran continued:

> — *First of all, we know that the evil ones are cowards and have no feel for compassion, decency and morals. These characteristics make them difficult to fight, because they know no restraints and therefore won't engage in any form of fair fight. Those characteristics also make them cruel, ruthless leaders even against the very people they are supposed to support. Actually, they are monsters, under a lamb fur whenever convenient for them, and—as the Keeper already pointed out—must be neutralized before they get any kind of real power!*

Some shouts of enthusiastic approval echoed throughout the meeting. One Ara commented to her neighbor: "No wonder that the Green Aras are called Soldier Aras..." The thus encouraged Soldier Ara continued, while showing his battle scars:

– Yes, I do know what I am talking about. Now, the question is, how to best deal with them monsters. I think we should do it in two levels: one for immediate results and a second level aimed at the future.

I would like to talk about the future first. Just killing the evil ones is no solution, because "neo-evil" ones will pop up again. Evil is forever, it will rise its ugly head whenever it sees a chance to become active and it will take different shapes, according to the circumstances. Mostly, to get to power the evil ones take advantage of a collective big worry, as we saw during the trees' sickness that lead to lack of food and then to hunger, anger and despair. In that occasion and now again, evil chose to yell "down with the bad inferior races, responsible for all present problems, up with us, the good superior race!" as its luring argument. There have been cases in other species, in which evil yelled "down with the bad wealthy people, responsible for all present problems, make wealth equal for everybody!" for luring the masses. Many other luring arguments we can't even imagine now may be criminally used by evil groups, making their early identification difficult.

But we know the danger signs: whenever we perceive **hate plus cowardice** *at one side and* **fear plus wishful thinking** *at the other, evil is around the corner. Action becomes then absolutely necessary, even more so when evil is addressing a big collective worry. Fear is not shameful; it is an important strategic instrument of living things to indicate the need for defensive action. Wishful thinking, on the contrary, is like opium. It is an expression of laziness that dangerously blocks the warnings sent by fear and must be energetically fought out. It is easy to defeat evil in its beginning and it becomes increasingly more difficult as its power grows. Therefore, it is very important that those in charge of educating and training the young, start to warn them about this as early as possible. Everybody should be able to immediately identify evil and to know how to fight it, including those not endowed with a bright intellect or a strong character.*

Any questions so far?

– Yes, I do have a comment, said a Blue-Yellow Ara. *You and many of the Aras here are making monsters out of those you call evil ones. I think that they are just Aras like us all, with some ideals that are different from the usual ideals. They are a small minority themselves and therefore a bit aggressive, to compensate for their limited numbers. We just have to talk to them and take some conciliatory steps, make a couple of small concessions to appease them... A* quite numerous group of Aras started to show signs of approval.

– Young man, interrupted the old soldier resolutely, thus stopping the approval signs, *you are being carried away by pure wishful thinking. As we saw before, experience shows that* **conciliatory gestures, concessions or any other form of appeasement won't stop those driven by hate. You have to effectively neutralize them at the beginning, or you will have to kill them later!** *This time definitely bigger signs of approval followed.*

The keeper of History then asked if there were more comments and a very young Green Ara addressed the old soldier:

— *You have talked a lot, sir, but didn't yet say how to actually fight the monsters,* which extracted some amused smiles.

— *You have to be a bit patient, son,* said the old soldier, not without some affection in his voice. *I'm now coming to that, because whatever we do to fight them monsters now, applies also to the PERMANENT fight we must sustain against the beginnings of evil.*

I have already mentioned that evil is forever. We may kill some evil individuals, but we cannot kill evil itself. It will exist as long as life exists in the universe. We can only contain it, keep it from spreading! This is the objective we will now pursue.

It is clear that the weaknesses of our enemies are our best allies. Evil ones always hate and hate makes blind and blindness makes at least a bit helpless, which leads to mistakes that finally lead to at least some stupidity that we can use against them on a case to case basis. But it is their cowardice that gives us the weapons to indeed neutralize them. Because of their lack of compassion, decency and morals they at first do intimidate and inspire fear, but before they get to real power it's all just hot air and if you confront them firmly with some backup power their cowardice wins and they retreat. By backup power I mean:

➤ *Good Aras that can fight or groups of good Aras that outnumber the groups of evil Aras.*

➤ *Good, brave talkers that can engage the bad Aras in discussions that smash their stupid arguments, laying bare the reality behind these arguments.*

➤ *The full power of our rules and traditions energetically applied, with very strong punishments whenever necessary.*

➤ *Increase of the effectiveness of the backup power by confronting the evil ones and their followers/sympathizers individually. They are basically weak and very much at a loss without their pals.*

➤ *Combinations of good fighting Aras and/or great numbers of good Aras with good talkers, in teams that interfere in the evil Aras' demonstrations and their other events. The fighters and/or numerous good Aras will stop physical violence and the good talkers will make it clear to the masses the stupidity and hidden cruelty of the evil ones.*

I stress again that all this is quite easy at the beginning but increasingly difficult later. If the evil ones manage to achieve real power, then only a battle can crush them.

At this point I must call your attention to a very small group of evil ones that are the famous exception that confirms the rules and are no cowards. They are fanatics, actually mad. They will ruthlessly kill, for absurd reasons concealed in their sick minds, mostly acting alone. They are easily manipulated and used by the cleverer cowards. Very often, they kill themselves after their murdering. These individuals must be simply killed. If duly identified, ahead of their attacks. Nothing else could effectively protect innocent Aras from them.

Now I would appreciate your comments. Have I been clear? Any questions? Do you agree or disagree? Are there any further suggestions?

After a quiet spell, needed by everybody to let all that had been said sink in, a middle-aged Green Ara, looking very practical and matter of fact, commented:

— *What you just said makes a lot of sense to me, sir. But who should carry out those actions, take the initiative, organize and coordinate them?*

— *I think that many people should become active,* answered the old soldier. *I actually see a big collective movement. For one, the Council of the Elders could designate some adequate Aras for this purpose. But, so could all sorts of groups, like spontaneous groups of friends, for instance. These spontaneous groups are ideal for tackling individual evil Aras and/or their followers, maybe in the group's own families or in their wider relations' circle.*

I see the fighting of evil as a missionary work of the greatest importance, which however, should be replaced by most forceful interventions from the Council of the Elders as soon as factual crime is identified.

Here the very same clever boy who had started the whole discussion posed anew a good question:

— *What do you suggest should be done if evil Aras take over the Council of the Elders?*

This time the Keeper of History answered:

— *Such situations have really happened in the past. As the old soldier has mentioned, when evil is in power the use of force, mostly a battle, becomes unavoidable. In a case like this, the danger of evil Aras not-in-power trying to mobilize the collective worry to allow them to replace the ones in-power is overwhelming. When fighting evil in power, the procedures we have talked about cannot prevent a battle but can at least prevent new evil from replacing the old one. That shows how especially important it is that those in charge of educating and training the young, start to warn them about this as early as possible.* **This is the best long-term strategy in the fight against evil.**

Among the Aras present was a relatively young Red lady, well known for her fine sense of humor combined with an extremely sharp mind. She had so far kept very quiet, but now spoke:

— *From what I heard and observed, the evil ones—like all weaklings—try to make themselves feared by faking courage and displaying their real lack of compassion exclusively against those who cannot defend themselves. A typical loud, hysterical shouting is part of their show. As long as they manage to be feared and thus to be taken seriously, they feel safe and self-confident.*

If we can shatter that fearsome image and ridicule them, they mutate in the Aras' general perception to just funny nobodies.

*First, we should find them a new name. The "evil ones" is actually supportive to the image they want for themselves, so I propose that from now on we all call them "dead moths", after the **death's head hawk moth**, a harmless but ugly moth with a perfect representation of a death's head on their back.*

©Olena1983 - Can Stock Photo Inc.

And then we should start to invent and spread jokes about the 'dead moths', like this one: A little boy go to his father, a very active 'dead moth' and asks if he can go out to see the solar eclipse that is just starting. "Yes" says father 'dead moth', "but don't go too near it!".

With a salve of roaring laughter, the crowd released the tension that had been developing during the long serious discussions, so different from their typically easy going, noisy late afternoon gatherings. Immediately, somebody asked for another such joke and the Red lady, very flattered and happy with her success, promptly reacted:

— *A passing by 'dead moth' asks a local Ara how long it would take to fly to the small lake at the foot of the hills you could see in the distance. The local Ara says: "Let me think…just a moment…". "Thanks a lot" says the 'dead moth', "that's great, I thought it would be much longer!"*

Another big laugh followed, but before more jokes could be requested the Keeper of History spoke to the humorist lady, who was now glowing with pride:

— *That was a great suggestion, love, and I hope it will be followed, and followed urgently. I am sure that wonderfully clever and funny jokes will start to circulate throughout the forest. But now it's already almost dark and the babies are starting to cry. We should go home.*

A few parents were starting to fly off to their offspring when a spontaneous chorus echoed. "one last joke, one last joke, one last joke". It silenced when our boundless humorist replied:

— *OK guys, I just had another idea that I will be glad to share with you. A 'dead moth' and another Ara were on top of a big tree enjoying its delicious fruits, when an 'urubu' vulture flying overhead discharged its bowls right on top of the 'dead moth's head. The 'dead moth', not knowing what had hit him and feeling there was something sticking to his head, turned to the other Ara and asked:*

"Can you please have a look and tell me what is on my head?". The other Ara looked and said "shit". The 'dead moth' said irritably: "I asked ON the head, not INSIDE it!"

And with this jolly piece of Ara humor ringing in their ears the whole bunch flew to their respective night quarters, laughing and talking, once again the noisy crowd we all love so much. But INSIDE their heads the inspiring ideas developed in that unique, remarkable late afternoon gathering were brooding and we can only hope that they will strongly contribute to neutralize the evil in their midst.

Bulli Beach
Paradise Found, A Friend Lost

After driving all around Australia, plus long detours to Alice Springs and the Uluru (Ayers Rock), Marianne and I were a bit tired and in bad need of some time to assimilate all the experiences and impressions we had gathered along the way. We felt that we had earned the right to a long, really cozy spell in Paradise (we were evidently not in a modest mood then...).

Naturally, by words association, Surfers Paradise was the first place that came to our minds. We had however been told that South of Sydney the New South Wales Coast was an insider tip, with beautiful, long sandy beaches and without the crowds we had seen lingering along the North Coast, especially in Surfers Paradise and Byron Bay. Therefore, after a visit to our great Aussie friends Judy and Terry, in Camden, already South of Sydney, on a glorious morning we proceeded along the South Coast. Believe it or not, in that same day, October 10, 2003, we did find Paradise, Down Under generally known as Bulli Beach.

The first night we spent somewhere inside the excellent local camping, but already next morning our chosen site became free and we could move in. It didn't take long for us to open the awning, turn the driver and co-driver seats around; put the table in between them and to connect external power, fresh water supply and wastewater discharge to a sewer. Removing

the garden furniture and our motorbike "Moby Dick" from the Garage and putting them to use was an easy, swift operation too. We soon found out that the periodic chemical toilette discharge could be easily performed in the nearby WC, using our folding hand cart for transportation. Later on we also discovered that internet Wi-Fi was available in the beach kiosk/restaurant where we would be eating most of our hot meals.

As for the superb location and view, I let the pictures speak for themselves, following the old wisdom that "a picture is worth a thousand words". And now you too know how Paradise looks like!

In this wonderful setting we fell into a comfortably relaxed routine. Marianne had planned to start cutting her films and I to work on my pictures, as well as to do some writing, but all this was not to be. At least not as much as we had expected. The path running between our camping and the beach was very popular with the tourists as well as with the Bulli folks (a bit more than 6,000), who used it for jogging and walks, including strolling with dogs, children and baby buggies. Our motorhome "Fuchur" was of an exotic type for Australia and so was our number plate, which attracted lots of curious people. They stopped for a chat and soon we had a bunch of friends who came by almost every day to say hello. In no time we, but mainly Marianne, had quite an active over-the-fence social life. I tried to tease her by saying that there were mainly elder gentlemen courting her, but her only reaction was a distant Mona Lisa smile…

However, not all our new contacts were done over-the-fence, nor were they all with members of the dominant species in this planet. Those who belonged to other species usually slipped under the fence to chat inside the camping:

A few times Judy and Terry came from Camden with their own RV, to stay with us for a while. A very welcome variation to our routine. Sometimes their grandchildren came along, lovely kids who brought with them a lot of life and laughter.

Our cores were shared between us as usual during longer stays in one place: Marianne cared for breakfast and eventual cooking, as well as keeping "Fuchur's" interior clean and tidy, while I looked after eventual maintenance and repair issues, as well as doing the "must" shopping with "Moby Dick". The daily needs Iike food, drinks, cleaning materials and so on, I bought from a small but very well supplied supermarket in the Bulli village, about ten minutes away. For more demanding purchasing I had a quite nice drive of approximately 12 miles (20 km) to the City of Wollongong, to where Marianne often came along (it seems that I am getting poetic…).

Wollongong, with something less than 200,000 inhabitants, is a highly industrialized but nonetheless very nice city. Nearby, at Port Kembla, are Australia's biggest steelworks. As a contrast to it, there are some great surf beaches, while towards the interior you find the most lovable landscapes. The city itself is very clean, the buildings all very well kept. Transit traffic bypasses Wollongong. For us, the main feature of that city was Crown Street, two blocs of which had been made into a beautiful mall, partially covered with an arched glass ceiling. Along both sides of the street are the shops, restaurants and cafés, all very inviting. Trees and flowerbeds add a pleasant note to the whole. By bad weather, fortunately seldom in that area, an ideal place to spend the day!

The Bulli supermarket had a different kind of charm. It was run by three very nice ladies in their fifties and exuded the atmosphere of the little general stores of bygone days. In my first shopping day there I had to fill our fridge and cupboards, so my purchase volume looked quite impressive. When I approached the cashier, occupied by one of the three managing ladies, then still unknown to me, she asked:

- *Are you the owner of that scooter outside?*
- *Yes*, I said
- *And how are you going to take all this stuff home?*
- *That's what that scooter is for.*

She gave me a stern look that clearly meant "one should not contradict psychic sick people" and just murmured:

- *If you say so…*

Well, after paying the lot, I pushed my shopping cart outside, parked it alongside good old "Moby Dick", which I proceeded to load. First the heaviest bags in the compartment under the seat and a big bag hanging from a hook in front; when driving this bag would stay between my legs. Then I placed a big bag, but not so heavy, on Marianne's seat and fastened it by means of a bungee cord. Finally the lighter bags went into the helmet box in the back and some smaller stuff I fixed, again with a bungee cord, onto a small rack on top of the helmet box. When I turned to push the shopping cart back into the supermarket, I saw that those three ladies had been watching me all the time and now stood there with their mouths wide open! One of them took the cart, I returned to the bike, started the engine, mounted by pushing my leg over the seat and the bag in front (I could still do it then!) and drove off. When I passed the ladies they started to applaud and I greeted them with a smile and a nod, the beginning of our friendship. When I told Marianne this story she at first laughed, then became serious and said:

– *I like that! You make silly remarks about my over-the-fence friends and what do you do? I'm the one who should be worried about your escapades!*

Since I knew there was no way I could ever win a discussion with Marianne and didn't even know how to make, like her, a distant Mona Lisa face, my only way out was to just overhear HER silly remark…

When not involved in the activities described above, we worked with films and pictures, read, swam, explored the surroundings on foot or just dozed. The hot meals, as mentioned before, we mostly took at the kiosk/restaurant nearby that also had some excellent ice cream for in-between the meals.

All in all, during six weeks, most of the time we thoroughly enjoyed that great Italian art of "il dolce fare niente" (the sweet doing nothing). At the end of this period we were feeling indeed very well and our old curiosity to see what's behind the next road curve took hold of us again. We decided to take a break from Paradise/Bulli Beach and to go exploring Australia's Southeast corner, which proved to be very rewarding, totally different from the country we had seen before.

We didn't return directly to Bulli Beach because we gladly accepted an invitation from Judy and Terry to spend Christmas/New Year with them, in Camden. For New Year's Eve however,

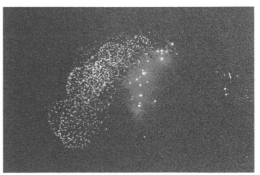

we all took the train to Sidney, where we enjoyed a picnic and watched the world-famous fireworks, an indeed magnificent spectacle!

On the train back to Camden Terry decided to show off with us, since we had learned to sing the unofficial Australia's anthem, "Waltzing Mathilda". He suddenly started to sing it as loud as he could and to prod Marianne, Judy and me into following him. To our surprise the whole wagon also followed and we had an unforgettable musical trip, full of Aussie patriotism and sympathy.

On January 2nd, 2004 we again occupied our beloved place at the Bulli Beach Camping. This time we would stay for about eight weeks.

Upon arrival, we felt like coming home and were soon back to our old routines. I have not yet mentioned that every morning before breakfast and again late afternoon, we went for a walk on the beach, followed by a swim. In the morning we  mostly swam in the big saltwater pool at one end of the beach, for safety reasons. In the afternoon the lifeguards  were generally present on the beach and we could then swim in the ocean. This brings me to the ocean dangers of which we had been thoroughly warned right after our first arrival in the camping. These were twofold:

First, sudden strong currents of unknown origin often developed along the beach, taking people away into deep water. This could happen anywhere, no place was immune. Those currents disappeared sometimes very fast but could also stay for a longer period of time, maybe even days. If you were caught in one of them, they told us, it was useless to try to swim back to the beach. The current was too strong and you would only endanger yourself by becoming totally exhausted. The best strategy was to let yourself be carried away until the current died out and then swim back to land. You could also try to get earlier out of the current by calmly swimming not against but across it. Anyway, the safest thing was to only swim in the safe zone between the flags set up by the lifeguards, where they had made sure that at least for the time being there was no current and where they were present to help you out, if necessary. No flags meant no swimming.

Second, sharks were liable to appear even close to the beach, a perspective that we found quite distressing, to say the least. But the Aussies had a solution for that: during normal swimming hours there was somebody observing the ocean from **a** small airplane and when he or she saw even one solitary shark fooling around, the lifeguards were informed by radio. They then shouted everybody out of the water, removed their flags and, depending on the hour, sometimes went home.

By the way, the lifeguards were very well trained for their job and had access to very adequate equipment, mainly: For each guard, on land a quad with a surfboard on it and, by the water a jet-ski trailing an attached surfboard. With the quad they could drive very fast to reach somebody near the beach and with the jet-ski they could reach in no time a troubled swimmer far out, who may then fix himself or be fixed to the attached board. The surfboards and jet-skis just floated over the water and were thus not easily carried out by a current, as long as not even a hand or a foot accidentally lowered into the water gave the current an object to grip.

For our late afternoon swim we always entered the ocean right in front of our camping place, even if we would then not stay between the lifeguard flags. In this case we just didn't venture into deep water and stayed where we could stand firmly on the ground, thinking that no current would endanger us there. A fatal mistake! One afternoon, a few days before our departure from Bulli Beach, we were already in the water, talking, only a very short distance from dry land. Marianne was floating on shallow waters just in front of me, looking towards the beach. I was looking away from the beach, standing with the water slightly above my knees. Suddenly I saw Marianne being slowly carried away without even noticing it. I immediately swam after her, to eventually help her out of the apparently weak current. But when I reached her, I noticed that both of us had already lost contact to the ground and that the current had become really strong. We were still very near to the beach and were both in good physical shape, so we started to try to swim back. But, as we had been warned, for no avail: we were getting farther and farther away from land and were becoming exhausted pretty fast. Marianne was the first to look for the lifeguards and saw that the flags were gone and everybody was out of the water, a sure sign for the presence of sharks! The lifeguards were almost ready to go home. She started to wave frantically and before I had time to grasp the situation and join her in waving, we saw that the lifeguards must have been watching us, because two of them were already starting their quads in our direction. In a couple of minutes they were jumping into the water with their surfboards and like a flash were with us. Each of us had then to lie down on one end of a surfboard, naturally making sure that no part of us touched the water. The lifeguards kneeled on the other end of the boards with only their hands in the water, paddling with them not against but perpendicular to the current, until we were out of it. Another few minutes and we were safe on the beach, thanking those guys effusively for actually saving our lives.

That night we spent huddling in a great hug, after a heartfelt prayer of thanks. Next morning we made a generous donation to the Lifeguards Organization.

Until this life threatening experience we had loved the ocean. We had both grown up with it, in an intimate friendship that we had further cultivated all our lives. Now it had betrayed us, even tried to kill us, showing its real double-faced character. From now on it was no friend anymore and we would treat it like the treacherous creature that it really is. There is a saying that "even in Paradise nothing is forever" and our adventure had proven it: In Paradise we lost an old friend indeed.

After the above described stress we had no further troubles and enjoyed life again until our departure. These would be our last happy Australian days. As part of its fight against terrorism, the government had ruled that starting at a given date no foreign vehicle could stay more than three months in Australia. Before this rule "Fuchur" had already been for about two years in that lovely country and now its last three months of legal stay were coming to an end. We would shortly be shipping it to New Zealand, ahead of new adventures.

The day we left we said a nostalgic goodbye to our over-the-fence and under-the-fence friends. I went to the Bulli supermarket for a last minute shopping and to also say goodbye to my three friends there. They came out to wave me away and as I passed them on "Moby Dick" one shouted:

- *And don't you dare ever to forget the girls from Bulli Beach!*
- *I won't!* I shouted back.

And I didn't. And now you, dear reader, you are my witness.

In the years that followed, Marianne and I saw many beautiful places, met many great people and experienced amazing adventures, but Paradise, on the maps mostly shown as Bulli Beach, always stood out in our memories and hearts as a very special Highlight.

On the Trustworthiness of Information

Brazil was very well known to us and the Brazilian laws only allowed for a foreign vehicle to remain in the country for a period of maximum ninety days. An additional extension of ninety days could be requested at the end of the first period but there was no guarantee that it would be also granted, and the bureaucracy involved was probably quite annoying. This was the reason why we had made Argentina our base in South America, for Argentina was the only country in that region that allowed an eight months stay for foreign vehicles after each and every entrance.

Thus, we decided to limit our visit to Brazil to the normally granted ninety days, concentrating just in the small part of that huge country that was new to us: the extreme South, the historical center and the Pantanal in the Southwest. The logical route was clear:

- Enter Brazil from Argentina, visit the state of Rio Grande do Sul with its beautiful mountain areas and its historical Jesuit Missions, as well as the interesting towns established by various groups of European immigrants.

- Drive North until São Paulo for a short visit to friends.

- Continue to the historical cities of Ouro Preto, Vila Rica, Congonhas do Campo and so on, in the central state of Minas Gerais. These cities had been once very rich due to the highly  productive gold mines in the area and to the precious/semi-precious stones flowing to their skilled jewelers from all corners of Brazil, a practice that continues even today.  In the eighteenth century many intellectuals fled political prosecutions in Portugal and established in the described area an important cultural center. In the resulting stimulating atmosphere, literature, philosophy, architecture and the arts thrived to surpass even Lisbon, making of these cities, in those days, the actual cultural capital of the Portuguese Empire. A Brazilian born mulatto architect and sculptor, Antonio Francisco Lisboa, nicknamed "Aleijadinho" ("Little Cripple" because of a serious sickness, maybe lepra) is now positioned in the same artistic level as Michelangelo.

– Through the fascinating Pantanal, the largest swamp area in the world, and the very enjoyable city of Campo Grande to the interesting city of Corumbá, at the Bolivian border.

– From Corumbá to Santa Cruz de la Sierra, in Bolivia.

– Exploration of Bolivia: La Paz and other cities, Inca and Spanish ruins, Andean Altiplano landscapes, Titicaca Lake, all internationally well-known places that demand no explanation here.

– Exploration of Peru's South: Cuzco, Machu Pichu, down the Andes to the coast, Nazca. Again, no further explanation necessary.

– Through the Atacama Desert in the North of Chile and over the Andes back to Buenos Aires, where, during our next yearly visit to Switzerland, Fuchur would be left once again. Between the Andes and Buenos Aires, we would be able to visit the university city of Cordoba, founded in 1573. In 1610 the Jesuits established there the Colegio Maximo, which in 1613 would become the fourth-oldest university in the American Continent.

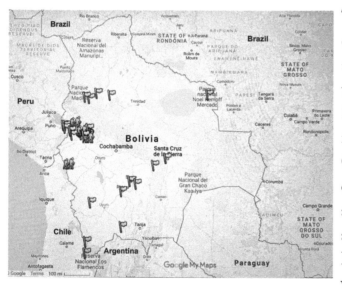

This highly appealing route was well enough documented in almost all of its extension and contained only one problematic stretch: the one running from Corumbá (Brazil) to Santa Cruz de la Sierra (Bolivia). We could not find any trustworthy information on it. On the contrary, the sparse data we got until our departure from Buenos Aires was vague and contradictory, varying from a completely asphalted road surface to a primitive sand trail. Even the total road length was inconsistent, varying between 500 and 1.000 km! In spite of this situation, we decided to follow the above route and try to obtain better information on the way, especially in Corumbá. If the road proved to be too bad or even non-existent, we could always return to Argentina through Paraguay and leave Bolivia and Peru for later, when we would hit the Pan-Americana Road to Alaska. We were indeed a flexible "young" couple in those jolly days…

The route until Corumbá met our expectations but we made no progress in obtaining better information concerning the stretch Corumbá-Santa Cruz. The nearer we got to the border the more we intensified our inquiries, especially by talking with truck drivers. Finally, in Corumbá we were told by several people that the road was already asphalted most of the way and was no problem anymore. Also, we heard, it hadn't rained for quite a while, so that even the unpaved stretches should be all right. Reassured by these clear statements from more than one source we happily proceeded West on Bolivian Road Number 4.

However, not without an initial stumbling block. On 22.02.2009 we arrived at the border to find it open but not occupied. Carnival was the reason and the border controls would remain closed until its end, on 25.02.2009. Only a couple of officials were there to check the passports, but to have them stamped we had to drive back to the Corumbá Police Station. The border customs office was simply closed. The passport guys suggested that we try to register "Fuchur's" departure from Brazil also in Corumbá, at the custom's main office. So, we turned around, payed once again the road taxes to and from Corumbá, got the passports duly stamped, but in spite of all efforts from the friendly, very engaged policemen, the customs office remained closed and no customs official could be found. We decided to just cross into Bolivia and settle the Brazilian customs issue, if at all, later, by mail. At the Bolivian side of the border, the same story. They also had carnival and what the Brazilians could do, they certainly could too… This time at least the Bolivian passport control people stamped our passports directly at the border and told us not to worry, because we could go through customs in Santa Cruz.

We drove all the way to the old Jesuit Town of San José de Chiquitos, where carnival was in full swing. The road, built recently by a Brazilian company, was in perfect state, completely asphalted, although without any infrastructure yet; no road signs, not even one single gas station.

On the way we had met Pires, a Brazilian from São Paulo, and a Japanese friend of his, heading to Santa Cruz on their motorcycles. As ourselves, they had gone through the same process of gathering misinformation about the road we were on now and had decided to risk it after reassurances from a friend of Pires who lived in Santa Cruz. Now, driving in that new asphalt road and not knowing what was still ahead, we were all positively surprised, relieved and in high spirits. Pires gave us the telephone number of his friend in Santa Cruz, saying that he may be interested in buying Fuchur for a "very good price". Fuchur was absolutely not for sale, but we were just a bit curious about the eventual offer.

We toured San José de Chiquitos, diplomatically avoiding the local booze and the spraying of Fuchur with different colors, both generously offered by the friendly carnival fans. The well-kept colonial architecture was indeed awesome. The church and its annexes, lavishly restored with financial support from Spain, greatly impressed us.

Because of the carnival, that attracted many people from a huge area, the few hotels were fully booked. There was no camping either, but with help from the police we were able to spend the night in the backyard of a small hotel, protected by its high walls and were even spoiled with power supply. We paid the price of a hotel room: USD 35. Some small children came visit us and left full of admiration for our good old Fuchur.

Next morning, we found out that not even in San José could we buy fuel. Based on the unreliable information available to us, we estimated that we had already covered more than half of the total distance to Santa Cruz. Since we still had ¾ of our total diesel reserve capacity, we were not really worried. Not so Pires and his friend: We heard later from them that in spite of having their motorcycle tanks filled up in San José, by a private person, for a horrendous price, they estimated that they still didn't have enough gasoline to reach Santa Cruz.

We had heard last night that shortly after San José the asphalt would end and that an unpaved but acceptable stretch of 140 km (87 miles) would follow. Now, before hitting the road once more, a young man spoke of 210 km (130 miles), but dry road… Marianne, in the driver seat, got us going with an open mind and much hope.

On leaving San José de Chiquitos we were stopped by an arrogant and silly policeman who demanded a road tax corresponding to about USD 20 and a bribe for himself that we finally brought down to USD 3.50. After that we drove on the asphalt road for a short time, when it was suddenly closed although nobody was working on it. We proceeded on an unpaved

auxiliary road, first parallel to the asphalt, then parallel to the not yet asphalted road work. Eventually the road work came to an end and so did the auxiliary road. Instead, we now followed a surface (not really even a path) incredibly full of potholes and partly covered with loose sand as well as long "washboard" stretches, ideally configured to dismantle the vehicles using it. We drove on and on for a long time, came then to some hills and got through them, frequently driving over big extensions of bare rock. After the hills the "road" returned to its former characteristics and remained so for a while.

Then, as a South African friend of mine would say, "the shit hit the fan": it didn't start to rain, it

started to pour! In minutes we were navigating in a sea of mud with the car trying to slide off in all directions. Marianne did a great job, keeping concentrated and calm. I cautioned her to go down to second gear and not to let the car stop, because then we may not be able to get it moving again. To block the differential and make things easier we would have to stop, which was a bigger risk than to continue our slow progress. Marianne was terrific, using the gas pedal with all the necessary feeling and keeping Fuchur straight by carefully countersteering. After many miles we finally found an elevation that was dry enough to risk a stop. Marianne was naturally exhausted and I took over. From then on, the blocked differential gave us a much better control of the vehicle. We had no choice but to push on and saw several trucks that had slipped from the "road" and now lied on their side, left and right of us. All the reassurance we needed…

Later on, we again met Pires and partner. Pires came toward us pointing out with gestures how he was covered by mud from head to toe and told us that they had been crawling along with

their motorbikes, both feet sliding over the ground, but even so he had already fallen five times. He was badly bruised, so Marianne pulled out our well-furnished first aid kit

and helped him to medicate his injuries, which lead me to call her "Miss Nightingale" (Florence Nightingale, 1820-1910, famous English nurse) for a good while... I'm really a naughty boy! Pires' friend had a flat tire and problems with his battery but was able to improvise solutions. We intended to drive on together, ready to help each other, but they had to part soon in search of gasoline in the nearby villages.

In the afternoon we reached an area inhabited by Mennonites, who had taken measures to make sure that the rainwater would drain out of the road, keeping it dry enough. The road was still sandy but well maintained, no potholes nor "washboards". We made good progress there and admired the nice farms with the perfectly tended fields. After overtaking a Mennonite on

a typical two-wheel, one-horse-drawn buggy, we stopped to ask him about the road. He was a very nice person, called Abraham and we had an interesting conversation. Abraham came originally from Mexico. Right now, he was transporting a gas bottle, showing that he was in some ways a modern Mennonite, although on the whole very traditional. The good road, he told us, would soon be finished and the mud would return as bad as before. He couldn't tell anything about the distance to the final end of the mud.

On we ploughed through more mud. It got dark and no end in view, the number of trucks laying on both sides of the road increased. Suddenly Marianne exclaimed: "Go right, now!" I did as she said, we drove a few meters uphill, out of the mud and stood in front of a gate to a very well-kept farmhouse. We opened the gate, drove through to the house and asked the administrator if we could park there overnight. He was

a very simple person and evidently much afraid of his boss, the owner of the farm, who was expected soon. Until his arrival we were to stay outside and only drive in when he allowed it. I told the administrator that this was not possible under the circumstances and that we would wait somewhere between the gate and the house. He should tell his boss that we just refused to go. After a light meal we went to bed and slept like stones the whole night, without noticing the terrible stink coming out of a cattle compound nearby. The owner never came, probably due to the appalling "road" conditions.

Next morning, I had a look at the car, because on the road, the day before, we noticed that the warning lamp for the foot brakes was glowing, although the brakes were working fine. On the other hand, the hand brake was slipping badly without any corresponding warning light glowing. Further, the front door on the driver's side was not working, but at least I managed to close it properly, important also because of the abundant mosquitos in that area. When I tried to open the motor hood to check the brakes, I found out that I couldn't do it, because the cable that actuated the lock had slid off and didn't work anymore… Underneath Fuchur all was covered with compacted, half dried out mud, preventing all access to the mechanical parts. We had no choice but to drive on until we reached Santa Cruz, praying that the lousy so-called road would not damage anything really critical.

It had rained overnight and was still raining in the morning. At 10:00 am the sun shone a little and we decided to wait for the "road" to dry a bit. However, after 11:00 am the rain came back and we left. The administrator told us that the asphalt started in about 15 km (9 miles). After a couple of miles, we came to a slightly uphill stretch approximately half a mile long, with deep trenches on both sides. The rain had washed out a dent in its middle which reduced the "road" width by one third. At the top end of this stretch three trucks were parked, indicating a mud-free spot. The truck drivers were standing there, apparently discussing how best to drive past the narrowed middle portion. We were already, as always on the mud, in second gear, so that I just gave some more gas and hoped for the best. We started the climb without problems and were nearing the narrowed middle section when a jeep showed up at the top, full of laughing young men, and without further thoughts, sliding left and right, drove down towards us at a considerable speed. Shortly above the narrowed section they managed to stop, practically in the middle of the "road" still idiotically laughing. We saw us already sliding out of the "road" but miraculously passed the dent and, barely missing it, the bloody jeep! Then for reasons unknown the engine died. I immediately restarted it, which fortunately went smoothly, engaged the first gear and with a minimum amount of gas got the car moving again. A fast change to second gear got us finally on our way. My only regret was that during the whole stress I didn't had a chance to tell those lousy s-o-bs what I thought of them. Not even a fist could I show them... On top we were received by the three truck drivers with a big applause. We stopped and stretched a bit, recovering from the shocks.

The drivers told us that the asphalt was only a few miles away. But before we could get on it a final test awaited us in the shape of a huge, very muddy road circle. It run around a dry "island" covered in low bushes. We approached slowly, in our permanent second gear and didn't know how best to navigate it: Clockwise or anticlockwise? Both sides looked equally muddy. On the opposite side, where the asphalt finally began, a truck was waiting to get in and we drove even slower to see which way it would go. But it was still on asphalt and we realized that its driver had all the time in the world, so he was waiting to see which way WE would go! We didn't want to risk stopping and in the last minute I just turned right and went anticlockwise, which fortunately worked out well. When we passed the waiting truck its driver greeted us very nicely and entered the same circular path we had come from, only in the opposite direction... But we were now safely on asphalt and in the mood to party, not to muse about sneaky truck drivers!

It was midday. That muddy nightmare had been 225 km (140 miles) long, including the short acceptable Mennonite road. Without all the wrong information we would had never risked it. But do you know something, dear reader? As a young South African adventurer once told us, "We were glad it was over, but we wouldn't have liked to miss it". The children that still lived in us were extremely thankful for that chance of living through an adventure that could have come out of  a Jules Verne book. We enjoyed every second and the stress was just an integral part of it all!

Due to the permanent driving in second gear with the differential blocked, we had a tremendous diesel consumption. And because, additionally, there was no gasoline station between Corumbá and Santa Cruz de la Sierra, this was the only occasion during all our trips in which we used up our whole diesel reserve, arriving in Santa Cruz practically on the smell of it. Back on asphalt we soon saw a very small, badly run-down gasoline station and decided to drive on, hoping for a more trustworthy one ahead.

A little further we were stopped by a police control, this time very nice people, that not only recommended a good gasoline station 40 km (25 miles) ahead, at the fringe of Santa Cruz, in a small town called Cotoca, but also gave us precise instructions on how to find the customs office to register Fuchur's entrance in Bolivia.

At the gasoline station we were told that because of the Carnival, the guy in charge of washing the cars was gone. However, the owner allowed us to wash Fuchur ourselves, free of charge, and we spent the afternoon on this impossible task. The mud had turned into a kind of cement and to make a long story short, it took us (and many Mercedes workshops afterwards…) more than a year to get it all off again. After a good dinner and a thorough bath we slept the sleep of the just in a quiet corner of that gasoline station.

During our car washing, I had noticed that the rubber stone-and-debris-catcher behind the right rear wheel pair was gone and Marianne had discovered a huge stone stuck between the same two wheels as the cause of a noise we had previously heard. These new acknowledgements completed the list of issues we had to tackle in Santa Cruz, which we started the very next day:

-   First, we went to a local Goodyear workshop owned by a Brazilian, where a tire specialist, also a Brazilian, removed the right rear wheel pair and then the stone that had been pressed between then, as well as several kilos of dry mud. All six tires were otherwise in perfect shape.

-   Second, we drove to customs, where a very nice young lady efficiently registered Fuchur's entrance in Bolivia but insisted on a fine of USD 25 for the illegal border crossing. Nobody is perfect…

-   Third, after lunch we went searching for a Mercedes workshop. Following one bad information after the other we finally had to give up and went to sleep again in a gas station, where the guard promised to keep an eye on us.

-   The owner of a vehicle's parts shop finally led us, next morning, to a Mercedes workshop. After much pressure from our side they agreed to take us in the following day and then managed all our repairs in two days. Before leaving for La Paz we called Pires' friend who, as expected, was not interested in buying Fuchur due to the huge Bolivian import taxes. But he told us that Pires, who had also managed the Road Number 4 and had arrived in Santa Cruz at the same day as we had, was with him and we drove by to say goodbye.

We had thus closed almost all issues connected with the critical stretch of our planed tour and felt like veterans of a great battle. Only the Brazilian side of the illegal border crossing was still unsolved, but we didn't feel like letting that detail spoil our good spirits. We were just excitedly entering the fascinating Andean World, new for us, and it was indeed the Corumbá customs that had irresponsibly left the border open. Only in La Paz, were we leisurely enjoyed the city, did I thought of sacrificing a little of the time we had generously given ourselves, to do something about that nasty pending matter. So, I called Corumbá and asked for the Chief of the Customs Department. I told what had happened and asked him to fax or e-mail us the confirmation that we had legally left the country, which he said he couldn't do. He wanted me to drive to the next available Brazilian border office and try to settle things there, an absurd proposal. A big senseless discussion followed, naturally without a solution.

We had entered Brazil through São Borja, State of Rio Grande do Sul, that had a big, very well managed customs. I then called the custom's Chief there and explained the whole situation. He was appalled by the open border during the whole carnival period and said he would start an investigation against the Corumbá customs. I was to mail him copies (not originals, that may be lost in the mail) of all concerning documents, including the Bolivian entrance ones, which I did. We then drove on, finished our tour as planed and flew to Switzerland, where the first e-mail we got was from São Borja, with the documents legalizing "Fuchur's" departure from Brazil enclosed. In the very nice e-mail text, the custom's Chief asked us to please never do this again but, in a similar case, try to find another solution, because we couldn't possibly imagine how much work it had cost him to get this through…

This was Brazil as we loved/love to our deaths, with all its human flair, its contrasts in nature as in the character of its people. The people in which I was born and with whom I grew up, far away from all discrimination and intolerance, that later received my foreign wife as one of their own, so that she always said that in Brazil she had spent the best years of her life. The country of the famous "jeitinho Brasileiro", that typical way of creatively managing problems around the cliffs of life to a satisfactory solution, as in the present case.

Pachyderms

It takes about two hours to drive the 153 km (95 miles) from Pretoria, the South African capital, to Sun City, often referred to as South Africa's Las Vegas. Well, this reference is very generous, and I prefer to stick to the facts: Sun City is just the biggest gambling resort in South Africa, maybe in all of Africa. It is nice and cozy for such a place, but Marianne's and mine real interest rested on the 500 square kilometers (124,000 acres) that surround it; the PILANESBERG NAIONAL PARK.

This park comprises an extraordinarily rugged area characterized by several extinct volcanoes and covered with a scraggy vegetation. It is however home to a wide variety of African fauna that usually keeps not too far away from two main water holes. This and the sparse vegetation make it relatively easy to find and to observe the animals. For us this National Park proved to be the best we ever visited, allowing for an unrivaled, intimate insight into Africa's wildlife.

The Park opened at 5 am and closed at 7 pm. Visitors were not allowed inside during the night, but during the day cars were permitted to be driven around or to be parked at will, under the conditions that the entrance fee had been duly payed and nobody left the car nor exposed any part of their bodies outside of it. Apparently, some of the permanent inhabitants of the Park were not to be trusted as food was concerned…

Adjoining the Park was a big camping where we spent the four nights we stayed at Pilanesberg. We always left the Park shortly before it was closed for the night and were already waiting in front of the gate when it was opened next morning. Breakfast we had while observing the life around a water hole and later, when things were quiet about us, we took a good nap. "Those were the days my friend", sometimes we had to pinch each other to make sure that we were not dreaming!

The first amazing insight in the lives of the African fauna we had in the very first night at the camping. To the Park belonged a relatively small water hole that could be very well observed from inside the camping, over a fence. We went to have a look and found quite a crowd already gathered there, observing a huge rhinoceros approaching the water. Then, out of nowhere a second, a little smaller rhinoceros appeared. They both stopped to look at each other in a not exactly friendly way. While they mused about how to proceed, a third rhinoceros, again a huge one, materialized out of the dark. What followed was strangely familiar. It was evident that none of the three rhinoceros had a clear concept of how they should approach the water. Foremost was the question of status: nobody wanted to be the last to drink nor the one with the worst place by the water hole. The "discussions" went on and on for over one hour. Sometimes it looked as if physical violence was about to break out, but it never happened. Often, they just stood there looking mistrustfully at each other. Then two seemed to make an alliance against the third one, which however never lasted long. Finally, they did agree on a certain distribution around the water hole and all started to drink at about the same time. Each one left whenever his thirst was quenched and went his separate way to deal with his own affairs.

We, the humans, were quite fascinated by those negotiations and couldn't help laughing a lot about the familiarity of it all. We soon realized that we had often seen exactly the same behavior in the daily news, when party politics and conflicts between nations were being discussed. We all saw that even our extremely distant relatives are indeed very much like us… Unfortunately, Marianne and I were not properly equipped for filming or taking pictures in a very dark environment.

The second great insight during our stay in Pilanesberg happened two days later and was even more astonishing in its similarity to us humans. One morning we once more crossed the entrance gate exactly when it was opened and headed to the nearest big water hole, where we found a good parking place, a bit elevated, offering a wonderful overview towards said water hole. We then immediately stopped the engine and proceeded to keep as quiet as possible, in which Fuchur's outstanding sound isolation proved once more to be a great asset. Following the by then established routine, we had our breakfast while keeping an eye on the water hole area. The usual customers were all there: a couple of lions, all sorts of antelopes, some wart hogs, and so on. Again, we marveled at their wise peace agreement: for good measure the antelopes and others mostly kept a distance from the lions, but they were indeed feeling protected while staying in the surroundings of the water hole.

Suddenly a big group of female elephants, with a lot of babies, appeared, led by a huge, evidently elder and very experienced matriarch. They were well organized and disciplined. They divided themselves in smaller groups that went, one after the other, first to drink at the water hole and then up a small hill covered by some lush bushes with evidently very tasty leaves, that they thoroughly enjoyed. The matriarch however did not go up the hill but remained looking back in

the direction they had come from, apparently worried or irritated. She then went some way back in that same direction, stopped and started to nervously bounce from one foot to the other, while silently calling, again to where they had come from (it is known that

elephants can emit sounds of frequencies outside our hearing spectrum). We were puzzled.

At once a teenager elephant came into view, nonchalantly walking with that same typical sloppy gait we all sported as "teenies". Then he saw the matriarch and all his self-confidence evaporated. He went to her and we could clearly see him trying to make excuses and saying he was sorry for the delay! She certainly did not let it go that easily and gave him some sharp reprimand. He then ran as fast as he could to the water, drank hastily and ran again up the hill to the others. The matriarch uncannily reminded me of one of my lady teachers at primary school and all my sympathy flowed to that "teeny" elephant: I knew exactly how he felt…

A whole bunch of more "teenies" followed, mostly in groups of two to five, and every time the same story was repeated (due to the distance and to the unfavorable angle our pictures and film are lamentably useless; fortunately, at least we had field-glasses). When finally all the missing little rascals were back home the matriarch went herself up the hill to her well-deserved breakfast. And we were once again aware of our close relationship with the other species on our planet.

We have thus met a group of female elephants with the young ones. Maybe not everybody knows that the male elephants must leave the group when they come of age. Onwards they live either in their own, mostly small group or, very often, alone and only come to the ladies during the specific mating period. They are then very irritated and aggressive. We had the opportunity to make the acquaintance of one of those elephants, however in another place, the famous KRUGER NATIONAL PARK.

We were driving along one of the many Park roads when we saw a huge male elephant peacefully eating leaves from some small trees just by the road. Naturally we stopped. He had his back to us, but he turned around immediately and quite clearly didn't like what he saw. As the encounter unfolded, we got the impression that he saw our good old Fuchur as a big white elephant, a powerful competitor. He approached us slowly, trying to show how strong and powerful he was. When he was already very near, Marianne, who had left the driving seat looking for a better angle to film, opened a side window that rotated upwards. Our new acquaintance must have seen it as an ear movement of his white competitor that meant a provocation. He then gave us a ferocious look and turned to fell a small tree by sheer force, which he did, in a clear power demonstration. As Marianne and I have always been peaceful people, but very resolute when provoked, we took the flash decision to immediately get the hell out of there...

A Magic New Year's Eve

In Earth's driest desert, the Atacama, in the North of Chile, two very different towns defy that harsh environment: The well-known San Pedro de Atacama and its much bigger but less famous, about 70 miles (110 km) distant neighbor Calama.

San Pedro is a very old historical city. During the Inca times it was an important stop for the traffic between the mountains and the coast. At the end of the 19th and beginning of the 20th century it became a stop for the cattle being driven from Argentina to the nitrate mines in the desert. It has a privileged location, at the center of one of the most impressive landscapes of Chile's North, near geysers, extraordinary rock formations and the largest salt flat of the country, in which a huge red flamingo population thrives. Nowadays San Pedro is the main tourist attraction in the North of Chile, offering a great number of very attractive tours, beside a laid back, cozy atmosphere. With only about 5,000 permanent inhabitants, it is indeed totally overflown by the several tens of thousands of tourists every year.

Calama, on the contrary, is a much bigger, young copper mining town, with a population of about 140,000 inhabitants. It lies west of the Pan Americana Road, very close to it. The Calama population is known for its pride, which they display by lavishly beautifying their town with all sorts of copper artwork, such as a copper plated spire on their cathedral, copper statues and copper wall decorations.

During our travels around Southern South America, we had driven a couple of times through that part of Chile, had visited San Pedro de Atacama but not Calama. This gap we were going to fill later, before leaving Chile for the last time, in a truly unforgettable way.

Before I come to that, I must point out that in spite of their differences, San Pedro and Calama are closely united by an important common factor: the desert and its sky. The clear, cloudless sky, the absence of big cities and other light sources as well as the stable wind, constantly blowing from the Pacific without turbulences, combine to make Northern Atacama one of the world's best platforms for astronomical observation! Not only for the many huge international observatories located there but also for amateur astronomers from everywhere and for romantics like Marianne and me.

On November 18, 2009 we departed from Quellón, South Chile, the official beginning of the Pan Americana, along which we were later to reach Fairbanks, Alaska. Already at the beginning of that trip, before entering the Atacama Desert, our faithful motorhome "Fuchur" signaled a couple of small issues that I considered taking care of in some good Chilean workshop, before moving into countries

with less mechanical resources. In our list I found a Mercedes Benz workshop in Calama, directly on our route. We arrived there in the late afternoon of December 28 and had "Fuchur" checked/fixed during the following two days. The workshop manager allowed us to live this whole time, two days and three nights, in the car, inside the workshop's premises.

In the morning of December 31, before leaving, we asked the manager if we could also spend the next night, New Year's Eve, there. We wanted to enjoy that occasion in Calama but were a bit worried because we expected that lots of drunken subjects would be around. He excused himself and said that their insurance conditions didn't permit us to stay inside. However, he suggested that we park for the night directly in front of the gate and he would instruct the security guard to keep a keen eye on us. This was a very good proposal that we accepted with many thanks. The workshop was a relatively small building inside a big piece of land, totally surrounded by a high wire fence, through which there was a practically free view. We would therefore be clearly visible to the guard even during his night rounds around the workshop.

Thus, relieved of all worries, with the car well prepared for the Pan Americana, we drove to downtown and, after a good look around, parked at a big mall with a good air conditioning system, where we escaped the considerable heat and pleasantly spent the rest of the day, without forgetting to buy the champagne for midnight.

Before it got really dark, we drove back to Mercedes, parked as agreed in front of the gate and I went to check with the security guard that he would keep an eye on us, which he confirmed. I returned to Fuchur and about 15 minutes later the guard knocked at our door. He said that he found it unacceptable that we could not stay overnight inside the fence and had therefore called the manager about it, but without success because of the insurance. He was sorry, he said. We thanked him effusively and explained that we understood the situation very well and were happy if he just looked after our security once in a while. He left still apparently quite unhappy but returned soon enough with a big smile in his face. He had called the owner of the workshop, who fully agreed with him, didn't give a damn about the insurance company and had authorized our overnight stay inside the fence!

We drove in and found a good place, with a magnificent view to the desert and with the lights from Calama behind us. In the dark, the wire fence was practically invisible, allowing a perfect view of the desert and anyway, we could admire most of the sky over the fence. As soon as we had ourselves well settled, Marianne and I went to the guard and invited him to stay with us for the years' passage. He was very touched but explained that he was on duty and only permitted to leave his post for the control rounds. Marianne then prepared a wonderful Christmas Plate, with cookies and chocolate from Switzerland, that we both took to him. This time he was really touched and had wet eyes. He said that he would taste a bit of everything but all the rest he would keep for his family. We were also extremely touched and grateful for having met such a good person, who had in fact, in his own modest way, a great soul.

We had parked so that we could see the desert and the sky from inside the car, where our fans kept us cool. We made ourselves comfortable, prepared the champagne and a can of salted cashew nuts for midnight, made some jolly tea, fetched the cookies to go with it and relaxed, slowly taking in the indescribable beauty of the sky and of the landscape before us.

As our eyes adapted to the dark, the desert became more and more visible. We could not see the moon that was out of our field of vision, thus slightly illuminating the desert without disturbing our extraordinary view of the sky.

The sky… Never before or after that night did we see so many stars at once. The star density along the Milky Way was so great that at some places they built cloud-like clusters in which the individual stars could not be spotted. That incredible sky hung like a canopy over the desert and both together created a magic, indescribable world around us. We felt as small as small can be in the face of an infinite universe, but at the same time we felt as an integral part of that universe, somehow happy and complete. I believe that in those magic moments we felt God's presence as much as we humans can, with our limited sensorial possibilities. And we were, as I still am, infinitely grateful for that.

We almost missed midnight and our champagne. Next morning, we crossed the border to Peru and set forth our Pan Americana adventure.

The following picture gives a rough idea of our surroundings that night but, unfortunately, no photograph can ever really convey the unforgettable magic we experienced in that bygone night at the Atacama Desert, in the North of Chile.

The Fable of

The Young Dolphin and his Friends

Along the East Coast of New Zealand's North Island, a young Dolphin boy was growing up under the loving care of a wonderful mother. He was extraordinarily clever for his age and prone to thinking ahead. Now he was starting to become more independent and to move around alone, not only inside his pod but also for short escapades outside it. Intelligent and extrovert, he was making friends everywhere. Among his new friends was an old man called Mowgli, who lived alone in a little hut on a small island, at a considerable distance from the coast.

Mowgli used to fish from the tip of a reef right in front of his hut, where the ocean was quite deep, and it was there that he and the young Dolphin had met. Mowgli had arrived in his islet some time ago and said that he was from a place he called India. He said that he came from a wolf's family (nobody really understood that), had been in many places around the world and was now retired. The fact is that he had a very big, loving heart and was very, very wise, evidently the result of the experiences gained along an adventurous and long life. He had been well accepted by his neighbors. To the philosopher Tuatara, the sly Crab, the sensible Seagull, the clever Owl and the incredibly old, wise Reef he was now connected by a deep friendship.

The young Dolphin knew that it wouldn't be long before he was fully grown up and bound to take responsibilities for the sake of his pod. Thinking forward—as was his character—and determined to make his mom one day very proud of him, he started to ponder about his future strategy for life. How was he to handle himself? How best to face all the varied situations in life, the expected and the unexpected ones? Actually, he only knew that he wanted to be successful, but also honest, truthful and supportive. His mom and several elder members of his pod had given him some hints, but nothing even remotely like a strategy and his life experience was too short to provide any basis for that. And so, he decided to talk about this with Mowgli, who seemed to be the wisest being he had yet met, and also a very kind one. On a beautiful, sunny morning he told his mom not to worry if he was gone longer than usual, because he was planning an extended visit to his new friend Mowgli.

As he had hoped for, he found Mowgli fishing in his usual spot, happy with the visit of his young friend. The boy always surprised Mowgli with his enthusiasm, curiosity and all sorts of intelligent thoughts. But nothing could have prepared the old man for the conversation that was to follow now.

- *Good morning, Mowgli*, shouted the Dolphin. *How are you today?*
- *How could I feel less than great in such a glorious morning? And you, how are you doing, my friend?*
- *The same as you. But I have to ask you something important!*
- *Alright, go ahead.*
- *How do you manage to live a happy, successful, productive life?*
- *First of all, you don't assault an old man in such a beautiful morning with the most difficult question in the world!*
- *Oh, sorry for that. Shall I return some other time?*
- *No worries, boy. It was just a joke. Back to your question. Give me some time to think this over...*

Mowgli mused for a while, as Dolphin swam around, looking for some edible fish, until Mowgli talked again:

- *What you are asking me for, dear friend, is a strategy. A method to follow. But life is very complex, and one method alone does not cover all different situations and aspects we have to face along the way. Important is that for each strategy you have a compass pointing in the right direction. A reference against which you can measure your position, how near to or far from your objective you are.*

At this moment the Tuatara, who had been discreetly following the conversation from a shadowy corner of the Reef, decided to come to Mowgli's help:

— *This is very wise, he said. And the first compass you need are your own feelings, so* **don't do to others what you don't want done to yourself!** *This is a clear strategy, easy to follow, that will keep you in the right track. It will encourage sympathy, friendship, support, and cooperation. Unfortunately, it can't be followed when you have to defend yourself against aggression.¨*

— *Exactly,* said the Crab, a fighter by nature, who had been attracted by the discussion. *In case you are under attack*, he added, *fight back if you can, doing to the attacker what he did to you. We call it* **tic for tac***. Your compass in this case is the aggressor's behavior. If the attacker, however, is too strong for you, run away and look for help, applying tic for tac later, after getting reinforcement from your pod or from some weapon or another strategy you devised.*

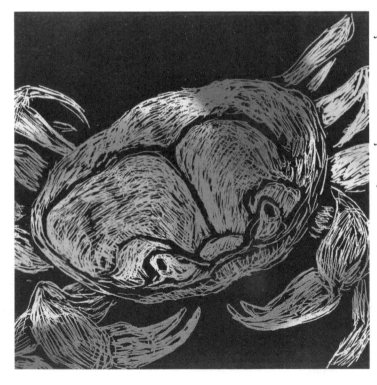

But, continued the Crab, *there is something you have to consider here: If your reaction (tic) is bigger than the aggression (tac), the conflict will escalate. If tic is equal to tac, the bickering will never end. So, if you wish to deescalate the conflict,* **your reaction (tic) must be a little smaller than the aggression (tac)***! Always remember this!*

Further, added the Crab, *as I hinted before, often tic cannot or does not have to immediately follow the tac. You don't have to react on the spot every time you are attacked, even if you have the power to do so! If, for instance, tac is only a provocation, take your time with the tic, prepare yourself well.*

— *Great advice friend Crab*, interjected Mowgli. *A great general–a human fight commander—pointed out once that "**a good general always determines time and place of the battle himself**"!*

— *Gee friends—remarked the young Dolphin enthusiastically—this sounds great! I have already learned a lot here! But there is something that has been troubling me lately. How about lying? Do I really have to always tell the truth?*

— The Tuatara answered: *This is a very awkward issue, young Dolphin, for which there is no generally applicable answer. It all depends on the circumstances; on the specific situation you are dealing with. Out of my lifelong experience I would say that you should always look for the real, the final truth and act according to it. Besides, if you know the truth, liars cannot fool you.*

However, TELLING the truth is an altogether different proposition. As a general rule, you should always tell the truth, because it keeps you and everybody else well anchored in reality, besides making you trustworthy. But be very careful about it, search your conscience and "gut feeling" every time. Sometimes a lie can be an act of compassion or part of a strategy for a worthy purpose. On other occasions, telling the truth can be dangerous, demanding a lot of courage, but is absolutely necessary. Still, when not COMPLETELY sure about the real need for a lie, do tell the truth!

As we can see, the number of participants in this spontaneous meeting kept growing and was now increased once again, this time by Seagull. This lady was an accomplished flyer and fishing specialist, who had developed a bunch of very successful tactics and strategies for her trade. Now she joined the meeting full power, as was characteristic for her:

— *Up to now you guys have dealt with behavior strategies concerning every day's life. Dolphin, however, also needs to be acquainted with a general strategy for a happy, fulfilled life, including keeping his belly full. The only really successful strategy for this that I know of, has to be carried out in **four steps**, starting with the identification of one's own strengths and weaknesses. Your strengths are then the compass to be followed. Whatever adds to them, supports your success.*

*The first step, therefore, is to **find out which is your real strength**. Compare yourself to others and see what is it that you can do better than anybody else around you. But don't stop at a general result. Narrow your search further and further until you find out what is really THE strength that only you have. For instance, don't stop at the fact that you are a great fisher. Go* *further to see why you are a great fisher, until you identify your speed or your reactions or your sight or your hearing or a combination of more than one of these factors as THE strength you are looking for. The more precisely you get here, the best it is for the steps that follow.*

The second step starts with a "don't": Don't try to improve on your weaknesses, it would be a total loss of energy. **Concentrate fully on improving your identified strength!** *Training, exercise, new and better tools, special tactics and so on, all it takes to make you gradually more skillful in the use of your identified strength. If one of your weaknesses, however, proves to be a real handicap, considerably impairing your skills, then you should make an exception and try to improve that too.*

As you improve your skills, make it known. *This is our third step. Find out who could use those skills and capture their attention. This may take some time, so be patient, but confident. Every skill is always useful to some user. Finding the user is your compass. To find many users means a big success, but few users can also bestow much success on a highly specialized skill. If you, for instance, can fish sardines to feed your whole pod, that's a great success. But if you, instead, are a specialized fisher of squids which can only be found a couple of times every week, it can still become a great success as a seldom pleasure for very special occasions.*

When you become successful, you have come a long way. But you have to make sure that you do keep successful, which brings us to our fourth step: **Become a partner to the users of your skills**, *by understanding their needs and constantly improving your skills in a way that keeps yourself able to satisfactorily solve their problems. This is your compass then. By the way, you often find some competition, but if you remain close enough to your users, systematically improving your skills in their interest, you are safe. Remember that you don't have to be perfect; it is enough that you keep a bit better than your competitors!*

At this point a new, very measured voice which, however, carried the sort of authority that only a superior intellect can cast, made itself heard: It was the Owl, the genius of that area. She said:

– *Friend Seagull, I would by all means add here an all-important fifth step. Success is of the essence, but if you don't crown it with* **HARMONY** *you will certainly miss happiness in life and even risk losing your success. It is in our nature of living beings that success tends to create envy in those less lucky in their existence. Not only that, but success normally confers at least a measure of power, which often induces arrogance, intentional or not. All this, if ignored, will fatally lead to opposition, conflicts and maybe even hate!*

So, Dolphin dear, when you climb the success ramp, make sure that you spread harmony around you. Always put yourself in the position of the others and try to understand what they think and especially feel. And then keep an eye on their interests as on your own. Hear them before deciding on issues that concern them and treat everybody with the due respect, which closes the circle, bringing us back to the beginning of this talk: don't do to others what you don't want done to yourself.

A short silence followed, interrupted by a deep voice that seemed to come from inside the earth, surprising everybody very much because it came from a source that was well known for its reluctance in speaking. It was the Reef and this time he indeed spoke:

– *Well, you all know, I am not fond of delivering speeches but what has been going on here has touched my heart. Lots of wise things have been said, with love omnipresent! I didn't even mind the big crowd stepping all over my head. OK, you know that I am very old, older than any of you can ever realize. I have seen beautiful things, like an infinite number of indescribably glorious sunsets, sunrises and starry nights. I also saw tragedies of an extent beyond imagination, like the death of almost all biological life on the planet, leaving behind a loneliness I could hardly cope with. That's why I should add one last very important strategy to the ones mentioned before, Dolphin: **Think ahead and think big, see what may be coming to you and prepare yourself!** There are events that you cannot face adequately or sometimes even survive if you are not ready for them. Maybe small events, like a resort for human tourists that may create problems to your pod, making it advisable for it to move. Perhaps very big events, like a climate change that may destroy your food sources, spear-heading the death of your people if you don't find in time a new source.*

The young Dolphin was completely overwhelmed by this flute of life wisdom, intellectually and emotionally. For the moment he was not able to talk. Mowgli then spoke:

– *I am tremendously impressed by what has happened here today. So much wisdom and so much love! I wish I had had such an introduction to life as you had now, my dear friend Dolphin. But you certainly deserve it. Before you return to your pod, I'll round out this meeting by reciting a poem written by my father a long time ago. (No, Seagull, my father was human. The wolves brought me up). This old but timeless poem ideally complements what has been said here. I just took the liberty of a little change in its last line, because my father was a child of his time and wrote it with men in his mind, whereas the poem is also valid for women, children and all beings of Creation. I am sure friend Dolphin, that with your privileged brain you'll be able to memorize it for life, as I myself did. And Mowgli recited:*

If

Rudyard Kipling - 1865-1936

If you can keep your head when all about you
   Are losing theirs and blaming it on you;
If you can trust yourself when all men doubt you,
   But make allowance for their doubting too;
If you can wait and not be tired by waiting,
   Or, being lied about, don't deal in lies,
Or, being hated, don't give way to hating,
   And yet don't look too good, nor talk too wise;

If you can dream—and not make dreams your master;
   If you can think—and not make thoughts your aim;
If you can meet with triumph and disaster
   And treat those two impostors just the same;
If you can bear to hear the truth you've spoken
   Twisted by knaves to make a trap for fools,
Or watch the things you gave your life to broken,
   And stoop and build 'em up with wornout tools;

If you can make one heap of all your winnings
   And risk it on one turn of pitch-and-toss,
And lose, and start again at your beginnings
   And never breathe a word about your loss;
If you can force your heart and nerve and sinew
   To serve your turn long after they are gone,
And so hold on when there is nothing in you
   Except the Will which says to them: "Hold on";

If you can talk with crowds and keep your virtue,
   Or walk with kings—nor lose the common touch;
If neither foes nor loving friends can hurt you;
   If all men count with you, but none too much;
If you can fill the unforgiving minute
With sixty seconds' worth of distance run—
   Yours is the Earth and everything that's in it,
And even more, true dignity under moon and sun!

A great silence followed, until the young Dolphin suddenly started a series of jumps out of the water, performing enthusiastic acrobatics while in the air, exclaiming with great feeling:

— *Thanks, a thousand times, dear friends! This was really cool! I can't wait to tell my mom all about it!*

And he departed like an arrow, in search of his pod. Let's hope that throughout his life he will remember and successfully apply the great lessons of that day.

Afterword

Before closing this book, I wish to point out once more that during all those years in our motorhome "Fuchur" we had been in fact living as ecologically as possible with the technology then available.

In our living quarters we used solar power for everything, except for:

- cooking, which we did by burning alcohol (a perfectly ecological process) and
- heating, which we did by burning diesel. But due to the highly efficient burners and to our extraordinary heat isolation, in cold nights we only had to activate the heating system for a few minutes. During the day, the car heater was more than sufficient.

Merely the car engine, running on diesel, was seriously non ecological. It was, however, the cleanest engine of that time, due to a turbo and to carbon filters, which we replaced regularly.

Our ecological footprint was by far smaller than the one of any contemporary home. With an electric vehicle, featuring batteries strong enough to briefly heat the car for the night, it is nowadays possible to further radically reduce a motorhome's ecological footprint.

Another issue I consider important to stress here, concerns our costs. We were in fact living mostly in countries with living costs lower than in Switzerland. Our flights to and from Switzerland cost the same as the ones that we would have had by yearly flying on vacation, if residing in that country. Only the shipping of Fuchur from one continent to another caused extraordinary costs. These, however, just brought us up to approximately the same total costs as we would have had if living in Switzerland.

So, all in all we had 12 years of a happy, high quality life, full of interesting people and exciting adventures, for practically no extra cost and as ecologically as possible in those days.

Acknowlegements

My deeply felt thanks to my Family and Friends, for their encouragement and support during the accruement of this book. A very special mention deserve my daughter Debi and son-in-law Peter.

Also to David Zeolla, Brenda McDonald, Melissa Weisberg and all the dedicated Dorrance Team go my sincere gratitude for their commitment and for the valuable advice they gave me along the publishing process of the first edition.

As for this second edition of the book, I am most thankful to Ethan Blaire, Maria Charmaine Ricafranca, Melissa Romo Martinez and the other members of the Authors Press team for their sound counsel and dedication.

Last but not least I wish to thank Jessie for the wonderful art with which she enriched my fables as well as for her honest and constructive criticism. She asked me to convey the following explanatory note:

Note from the artist of the fables' illustrations.

These images are directly inspired by Steffen and Marianne's fantastic art collection acquired through their travels. Also, my different choices of mediums/techniques, and style of representation were guided by the different cultures represented in each fable. Each set of images is meant to complement the storyline while also celebrating the diversity of the world we live in. Jessie Proksa

CPSIA information can be obtained
at www.ICGtesting.com
Printed in the USA
BVHW020229060222
627491BV00002B/5